W9-APH-769

THE HEALTHY BODY COOKBOOK

THE HEALTHY BODY COOKBOOK

OVER 50 FUN ACTIVITIES AND DELICIOUS RECIPES FOR KIDS

Joan D'Amico

Karen Eich Drummond, Ed.D., R.D.

Illustrations by Tina Cash-Walsh

JOSSEY-BASS
A Wiley Imprint
www.josseybass.com

Published by Jossey-Bass
A Wiley Imprint
989 Market Street, San Francisco, CA 94103-1741 www.josseybass.com

Published simultaneously in Canada.

Library of Congress Cataloging-in-Publication Data

D'Amico, Joan
The healthy body cookbook : over 50 fun activities and delicious recipes for kids / Joan D'Amico, Karen Eich Drummond.
p. cm.
Includes index.
Summary: Discusses the various parts of the human body and what to eat to keep them healthy. Includes recipes that contain nutrients important for the heart, muscles, teeth, skin, nerves, and other parts of the body.
ISBN 0-471-18888-3 (paper : alk. paper)
1. Cookery—Juvenile literature. 2. Nutrition—Juvenile literature. [1. Nutrition. 2. Cookery. 3. Body, Human.]
I. Drummond, Karen Eich. II. Title.
TX652.5.D344 1998
641.5'123—dc21 98-2776

Printed in the United States of America
FIRST EDITION
PB Printing 10

CONTENTS

ABOUT THIS BOOK

The Healthy Body Cookbook will help you learn more about your amazing body and what to eat to keep it fit and healthy. The introductory section, "Discovering the Kitchen," covers the basics about kitchen tools, cooking skills, and safety rules. Read it carefully before you do any of the activities or try any of the recipes.

The rest of the book is split into two parts. The first looks at the parts of your body: your heart, blood, muscles, bones, teeth, skin, hair, nails, nerves, and digestive system. The second explains how to keep your body healthy by eating right and exercising.

Each chapter begins by introducing and explaining a different body concept, followed by an activity to do. Each chapter then goes on to give you several delicious recipes that contain nutrients needed for the part of the body being discussed or for a healthy body in general. **Nutrients** are substances in food that are needed to make your body grow, to repair your body, and to keep you healthy.

easiest

intermediate

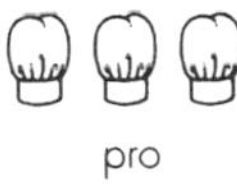

pro

Each recipe is rated according to how much cooking experience is required. The easiest recipes, marked with one chef's hat (called a toque), require no previous cooking experience. Intermediate recipes, with two chef's hats, require some cooking experience. Pro recipes, with three chef's hats, require the most advanced cooking skills.

Always be sure you have an adult to guide you when the activity or recipe asks you to use the oven, the stove, electrical appliances, or a knife.

These recipes also:

- list the time you will need to make them, the kitchen tools you'll need, and the number of servings each recipe makes
- use easy-to-find ingredients and standard kitchen equipment
- are kid-tested and kid-approved
- emphasize wholesome ingredients

At the end of the book, you'll find a glossary and sections on nutrition and food safety, including an explanation of how to read a food label. There's also a chart listing the nutritional values of all the recipes in the book.

So put on your apron, wash your hands, roll up your sleeves, and get ready to explore the human body. We hope you have as much fun learning, cooking, and eating as we did writing this book for you!

Joan D'Amico
Wayne, New Jersey

Karen Eich Drummond
Yardley, Pennsylvania

DISCOVERING THE KITCHEN

TOOLS OF THE TRADE

baking pan

colander

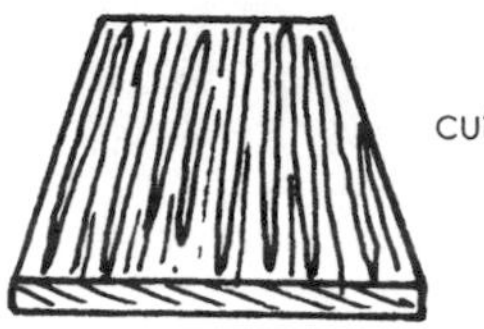
cutting board

biscuit cutter

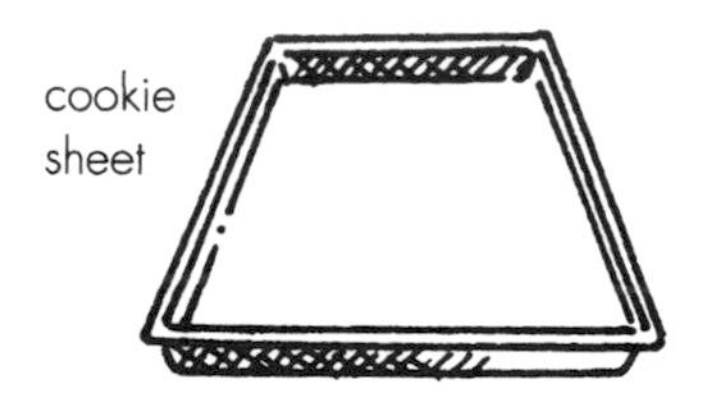
cookie sheet

electric blender

electric mixer

Let's take a close look at the cooking equipment in your kitchen. These are the basic tools you'll need to prepare the recipes in this book. Any kitchen tools that are used in only one or two recipes are described within those recipes.

baking pan A square or rectangular pan used for baking and cooking foods in the oven. The most common sizes are 9-inch × 13-inch and 8-inch square.

biscuit cutter A round outline, usually made from metal, used to cut biscuits from dough.

colander A large perforated bowl used for rinsing food and draining pasta or other foods.

cookie sheet A large rectangular pan with no sides or with half-inch sides, used for baking cookies and other foods.

cutting board Made from wood or plastic, cutting boards provide a surface on which to cut foods.

egg separator A small, shallow metal cup with slots used to separate the egg whites from the yolk. The yolk sits in the middle while the whites drop through the slots into a bowl.

electric blender A glass or plastic cylinder with a rotating blade at the bottom. A small motor in the base turns the blade. The blender has different speeds and is used for mixing, blending, grinding, and pureeing.

electric mixer Two beaters that rotate to mix ingredients together. Used for mashed potatoes, cake batters, and other mixing jobs.

grater A metal surface with sharp-edged holes used for shredding and grating foods such as vegetables and cheese.

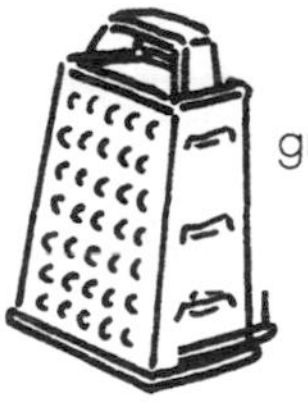

grater

knives:

- **paring knife** A knife with a small pointed blade used for trimming and paring vegetables and fruits and other cutting jobs that don't require a larger knife. (Most recipes in this book call for a knife. You will find the paring knife works well in most situations.)
- **peeler** A handheld tool that removes the peel from fruits and vegetables.
- **sandwich spreader** A knife with a dull blade that is designed to spread fillings on bread.
- **table knife** A knife used as a utensil at the table.

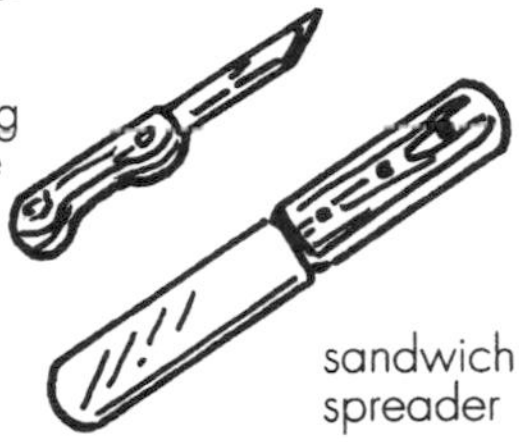

paring knife

sandwich spreader

layer cake pans Round metal pans used to bake layers of a cake.

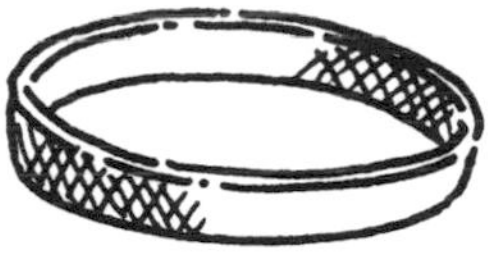

layer cake pan

measuring cups Cups with measurements (½ cup, ⅓ cup, etc.) on the side, bottom, or handle. Measuring cups that have spouts are used for liquid ingredients. Measuring cups without spouts are used for dry ingredients such as flour.

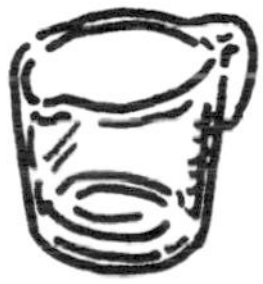

measuring cup

measuring spoons Used for measuring small amounts of foods such as spices. They come in a set of 1 tablespoon, 1 teaspoon, ½ teaspoon, and ¼ teaspoon.

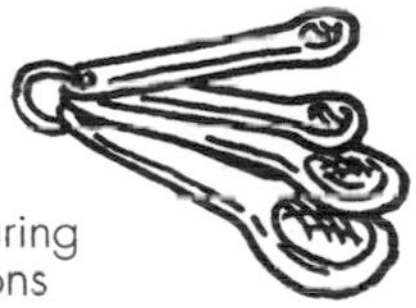

measuring spoons

microwave dish A dish that can safely be used in the microwave oven. The best microwave dishes say "microwave safe" on the label. Don't use metal pans, aluminum foil, plastic foam containers, brown paper bags, plastic wrap, or margarine tubs in the microwave.

mixing bowls Round-bottomed bowls used for mixing and whipping all kinds of foods. Depending on the amount of ingredients, a large, medium, or small bowl may be used.

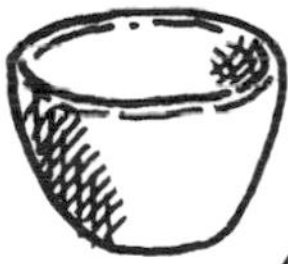

mixing bowl

muffin tins Metal or glass pans with small, round cups used for baking muffins and cupcakes.

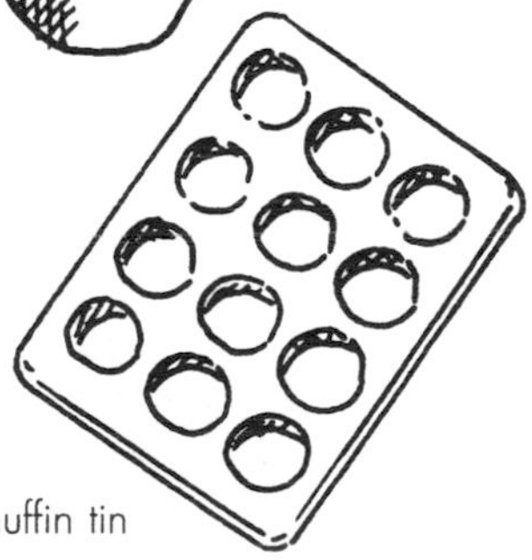

muffin tin

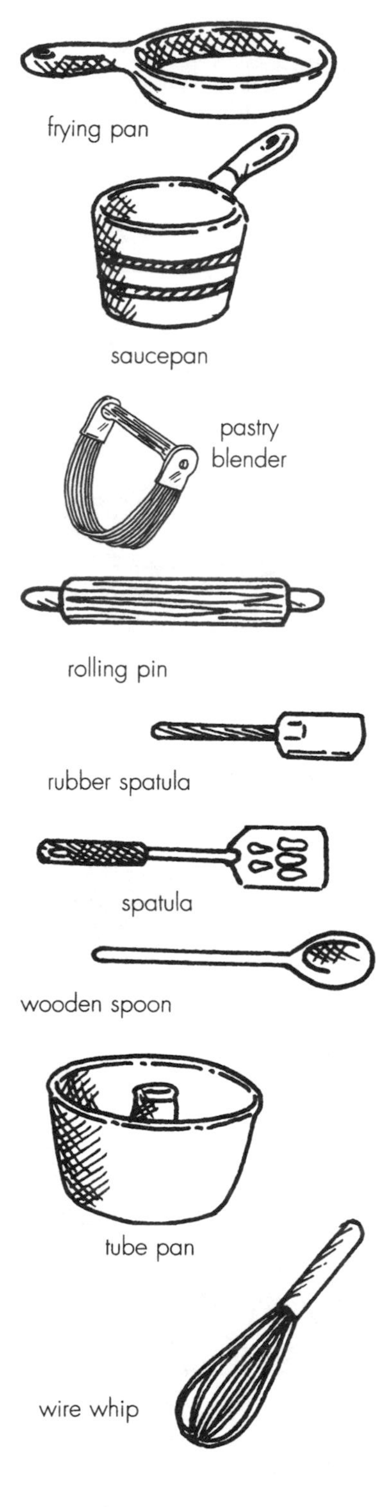

pans:

- **frying pan** (also called a sauté pan) Used for cooking foods, such as hamburgers or onions, in hot fat.
- **saucepan** (also called pot) Used for general stovetop cooking, such as boiling pasta or simmering a sauce.

pastry blender A group of stiff wires attached to both ends of a handle. It is used, with a rocking motion, to blend butter or margarine into flour and other dry ingredients to make a dough.

rolling pin A wooden or plastic roller used to flatten items such as pie crust and biscuit dough.

rubber spatula A flat, flexible rubber or plastic tip on a long handle. It is used to scrape bowls, pots, and pans and for **folding** (a gentle over-and-under motion) ingredients into whipped cream or other whipped batter.

spatula A flat metal or plastic tool used for lifting and turning meats, eggs, and other foods.

spoons:

- **teaspoon** A spoon used for measuring. Also the name for the spoon normally used as a utensil at the table.
- **wooden spoon** Used for mixing ingredients together and stirring.

tube pan A metal cake pan with a center tube used for making angel food cakes, bundt cakes, and special breads.

wire whip Used especially for whipping egg whites and cream.

wire rack Used for cooling baked goods.

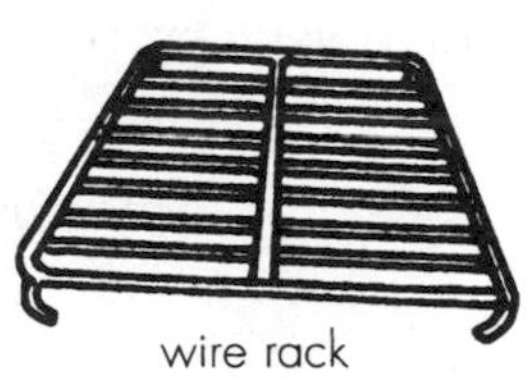

COOKING SKILLS

Chefs need to master cutting and measuring skills and the basics of mixing and stovetop cooking. Here are the skills you will be practicing as you try the recipes in this book.

CUTTING

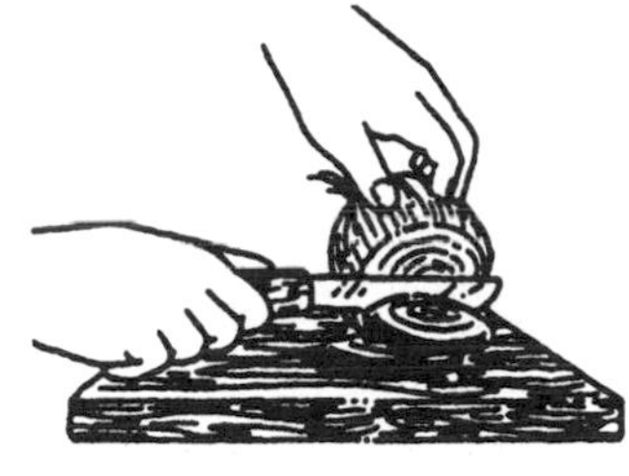

Foods are cut before cooking so that they will look good and cook evenly. Place the food to be cut on a cutting board and use a knife that is a comfortable size for your hand. To hold the knife, place your hand on top of the handle and fit your fingers around the handle. The grip should be secure but relaxed. In your other hand, hold the item being cut. Keep your fingertips curled under to protect them from cuts. (See the "Safety Rules" section of the introduction for more on how to cut safely.)

Here are some commonly used cutting terms you'll need to know.

chop To cut into irregularly shaped pieces.

dice To cut into cubes of the same size.

mince To chop very fine.

slice To cut into uniform slices.

Grating and shredding are also examples of cutting.

grate To rub a food across a grater's tiny punched holes to produce small or fine pieces of food. Hard cheeses and some vegetables are grated.

shred To rub a food across a surface with medium to large holes or slits. Shredded foods look like strips. The cheese used for making pizza is always shredded.

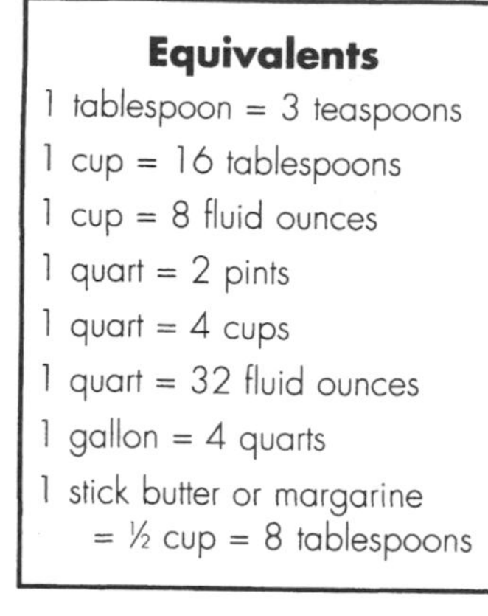

Equivalents

1 tablespoon = 3 teaspoons
1 cup = 16 tablespoons
1 cup = 8 fluid ounces
1 quart = 2 pints
1 quart = 4 cups
1 quart = 32 fluid ounces
1 gallon = 4 quarts
1 stick butter or margarine
= ½ cup = 8 tablespoons

MEASURING

Ingredients can be measured in three different ways: by counting (six apples), by measuring volume (½ cup of applesauce), or by measuring weight (a pound of apples).

To measure the volume of a liquid, always place the measuring cup on a flat surface and check that the liquid goes up to the proper line on the measuring cup while looking directly at it at eye level.

To measure the volume of a dry ingredient, such as flour, spoon it into the measuring cup and level it off with a table knife. Do not pack the cup with the dry ingredient—that is, don't press down on it to make room for more—unless the recipe says to.

MIXING

There are all kinds of ways to mix! Here are definitions of the most common types.

beat To move a utensil back and forth to blend ingredients together.

cream To mix a solid fat (usually margarine or butter) and sugar by pressing them against a bowl with the back of a spoon until they look creamy.

fold To move a utensil with a gentle over-and-under motion.

mix To combine ingredients so that they are all evenly distributed.

whip To beat rapidly using a circular motion, usually with a whip, to incorporate air into the mixture (such as in making whipped cream).

whisk To beat ingredients together lightly with a wire whip until they are well blended.

STOVETOP COOKING

There are different ways to cook on your stove. Here are descriptions of cooking methods you will be practicing as you try the recipes in this book. Because it is easy to get burned while cooking on the stove, see the "Safety Rules" section of the introduction.

boil To heat a liquid to its boiling point, or to cook in a boiling liquid. Water boils at 212°F. You can tell it is boiling when you see lots of large bubbles popping to the surface. When a liquid boils, it is turning into steam (the gaseous state of water). Water can't get any hotter than 212°F; it can only make steam faster. Boiling is most often used for cooking pasta.

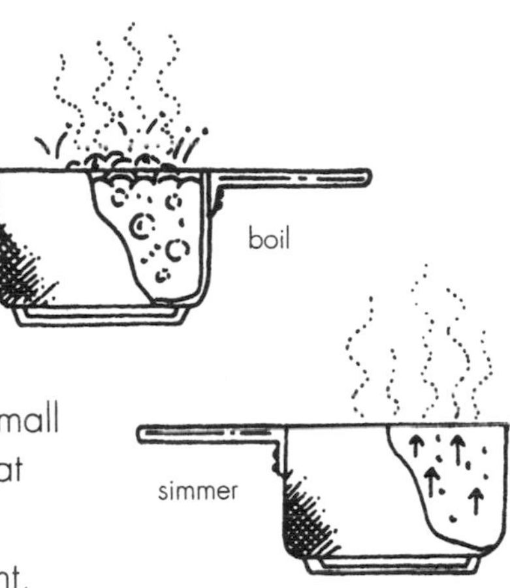

pan-fry To cook in a pan over moderate heat in a small amount of fat. Hamburgers are an example of a food that can be pan-fried.

simmer To heat a liquid to just below its boiling point, or to cook in a simmering liquid. You can tell a liquid is simmering when it has bubbles floating slowly to the surface. Most foods cooked in liquid are simmered. Always watch simmering foods closely so that they do not boil.

steam To cook in steam. Steam has much more heat and cooks foods more quickly than boiling water does. Steaming is an excellent method for cooking most vegetables.

sauté To cook quickly in a pan over medium-high heat in a small amount of fat. Vegetables, especially onions, are often sautéed in oil to bring out their flavor and brown them.

sauté

CRACKING AND SEPARATING EGGS

It is best to crack an egg into a clear glass cup (such as a measuring cup) before adding it to the other ingredients. That way, if the egg smells bad or has a red spot, you can throw it out before the egg goes in with the other ingredients. An egg with a red spot is safe to eat but is usually thrown out because of its appearance. You should also remove any pieces of eggshell from the egg before adding the egg to the other ingredients.

Sometimes you will need to separate the egg yolk from the egg white for a recipe. To do this, crack the egg over an egg separator and a bowl. Make sure you get the yolk in the middle. The whites will drain out into the bowl. If you don't have an egg separator, you can separate an egg by cracking it over a bowl, keeping the yolk in one half of the shell. Carefully pass the egg yolk from one half of the shell to the other without letting it break until the whites have all fallen into the bowl.

SAFETY RULES

The kitchen can be a safe, or a very dangerous, part of your home. What's dangerous in your kitchen? Sharp knives, boiling water, and hot oil are a few things. Always check with an adult before trying any of the recipes. Talk to him or her about what you are allowed to do by yourself and when you need an adult's assistance. And always follow these safety guidelines.

AROUND THE STOVE AND OVEN

- Get an adult's permission before using a stove or oven.
- Don't wear long, baggy shirts or sweaters when cooking. They could catch fire.
- Never turn your back on a frying pan that contains oil.
- Never fry with oil at a high temperature.
- Don't spray a pan with vegetable oil cooking spray over the stove or near heat. Oil will burn at high temperatures, so spray the pan over the sink.
- If a fire starts in a pan on the stove, you can smother it by covering it with the pan lid or pouring baking soda on it. Never use water to put out a fire in a pan with oil—it only makes a fire worse.
- Always use pot holders or wear oven mitts when using the oven or handling something that is hot. Make sure your pot holders are not wet. Wet pot holders transmit the heat from the hot item you are holding directly to your skin.

- Don't overfill pans with boiling or simmering liquids.
- Open pan lids away from you to let steam escape safely.
- Keep pan handles turned away from the edge of the stove. Knocking against them can splatter hot food.
- Stir foods with long-handled spoons.
- Keep pets and small children away from hot stoves and ovens during cooking. (Try to keep them out of the kitchen altogether.)

USING ANY APPLIANCE

- Use an appliance only if you know exactly how to operate it and you have permission from an adult.
- Never operate an appliance that is near the sink or sitting in water.
- Don't use frayed electrical cords or damaged plugs and outlets. Tell an adult.

USING A MICROWAVE OVEN

- Use only microwave-safe cookware, paper towels, paper plates, or paper cups.
- Use pot holders or oven mitts to remove items.
- If a dish is covered, make sure there is some opening through which steam can escape during cooking.
- When taking foods out of the microwave, open the container so that steam escapes *away* from your hands and face.
- Prick foods like potatoes and hot dogs with a fork before putting them into the microwave.
- Never try to cook a whole egg in the microwave—it will burst!

USING A KNIFE

- Get an adult's permission before using any knife.
- Always pick up a knife by its handle.
- Pay attention to what you're doing!
- Cut away from the body and away from anyone near you.
- Use a sliding, back-and-forth motion when slicing foods with a knife.
- Don't leave a knife near the edge of a table. It can be easily knocked off, or a small child may touch it.
- Don't try to catch a falling knife.
- Don't use knives to cut string, to open cans or bottles, or as a screwdriver.
- Don't put a knife into a sink full of water. Instead, put it on the drainboard, to avoid cutting yourself.

CLEANING UP

Whenever you use a knife and cutting board to cut meat, poultry, or seafood, be sure to wash them thoroughly before using again. These foods contain germs that can be harmful, and you don't want the germs to get onto foods that won't be cooked, such as vegetables for salads. Appendix C contains more information on cleaning up so food is safe to eat.

PART 1

YOUR AMAZING BODY

When you sit down to relax after coming home from school or playing a game, you probably think that your body is not very active. Well, there's really plenty going on! Even when your body is at rest, your heart muscle is pumping blood to all parts of your body, your lungs are breathing in fresh air, your bones are being built and rebuilt, your hair is growing, your nerves are communicating, and your digestive system is processing food that you've eaten. Read on in the following chapters to learn more about the fascinating activities happening in your body.

CHAPTER 1

HAVE A HEALTHY HEART!

In the middle of your chest lies one of the body's strongest muscles—your **heart.** About the size of your fist, the heart has to be strong because its job is to pump blood through more than 60,000 miles of **blood vessels** (tubes that carry blood) all day, every day. The right side of your heart pumps blood to your lungs to get oxygen. The left side pumps blood carrying oxygen to the rest of your body. The two sides of the heart are connected by **valves**—small holes that open and shut to let blood through.

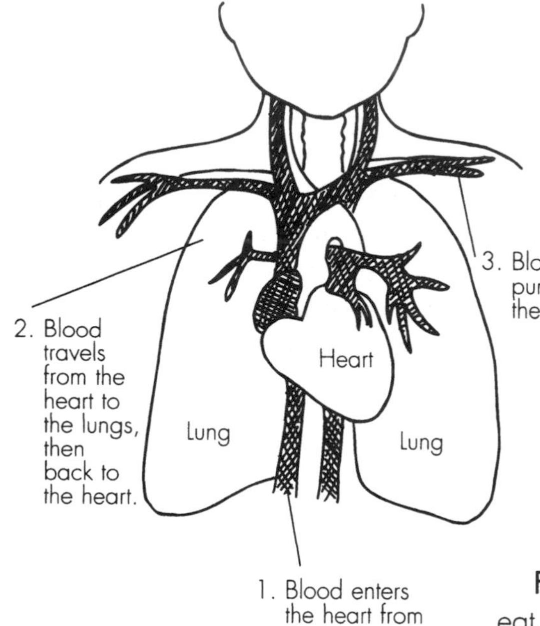

Just how hard does your heart work? That depends on what you are doing. Your heart beats each time it sends blood off to the lungs. An adult's heart beats about 60 to 100 times a minute; a child's beats about 90 to 100 times a minute. When you are excited or scared, your heart beats faster. When you exercise, your heart beats much faster and works harder so that your blood can take extra nutrients and oxygen to your muscles.

Your heart muscle needs nutrients and oxygen, too. It uses them to produce energy for its constant pumping. The heart muscle has its own system of blood vessels, called **coronary arteries,** that supply the heart with nutrients and oxygen.

Fat and **cholesterol** are part of much of the food we eat, and they have special jobs to do in our body. But too much fat and cholesterol in the blood can build up in the arteries, reducing the size of the opening in the arteries. If the opening in the coronary arteries becomes too small, not enough blood can get through, which can cause heart problems.

You can slow down or stop the buildup of fat and cholesterol in your arteries by eating right and getting lots of exercise.

To help keep a healthy heart:

1. Eat plenty of fruits and vegetables every day.
2. Feast on whole-grain bread, cereal, pasta, and rice.
3. Don't forget to drink your skim or low-fat milk!
4. Try frozen fruit bars, low-fat frozen yogurt, graham crackers, or pretzels as desserts or snacks instead of fatty foods such as ice cream, cookies, or potato chips.

Before you start eating right and exercising, do the following activity to hear what a heartbeat sounds like!

WHAT DOES A HEARTBEAT SOUND LIKE?

Purpose

To hear a heartbeat.

Materials

2 small plastic funnels
2 to 3 feet of rubber or plastic tubing
modeling clay about the size of an orange
helper

Steps

1. Push a funnel into each end of the tubing.
2. Break the modeling clay in half. Use each piece of clay to seal the funnels to the tubing.
3. Place one funnel over your ear and the other funnel in the middle of your helper's chest.
4. Listen for a heartbeat.

What Happened?

With your funnels and tubing, you made a tool used to hear sounds inside the body called a **stethoscope.** When you place the stethoscope against your helper's chest, you can hear his or her heartbeat. A heartbeat is the sound the heart makes when it squeezes together to send blood off to the lungs and to the body. Listen for the "lub-dub" sound the valves in the heart make when they snap shut with each heartbeat. One set of valves first makes the "lub" sound, then the second set of valves makes the "dub" sound.

The recipes in this chapter are all heart healthy, which means they are low in fat. So why not start with Braided Breakfast Cinnamon Bread for a high-in-taste and low-in-fat morning treat!

Braided Breakfast Cinnamon Bread

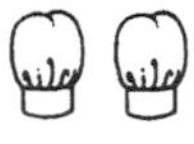

If you like to braid, this is the recipe for you. Using frozen bread dough that has been thawed, you cut the bread into three strips you braid just like you braid hair. It looks fantastic when it comes out of the oven, too.

Time
30 minutes to prepare
plus
45 minutes to rise
and
35 minutes to bake

Tools
cutting board
paring knife
cookie sheet
kitchen towel
2 small bowls
egg separator
fork
pastry brush
oven mitts

Makes
1 loaf (16 servings)

Ingredients

1 loaf frozen bread dough
1 tablespoon flour for dusting
vegetable oil cooking spray
¼ cup light brown sugar (packed)
1 tablespoon white sugar
1 teaspoon cinnamon
1 egg
1 teaspoon water

Steps

1. Allow frozen bread dough to thaw overnight in the refrigerator.
2. Preheat the oven to 350°F.

3. On a lightly floured cutting board, use the paring knife to cut the bread dough lengthwise into 3 strips.
4. At one end of the loaf, press the 3 dough strips together to join. Begin braiding, using these instructions. Spread out the three strips of dough. Cross the right dough strip over the center dough strip. Then, cross the left dough strip over the center dough strip. Continue this process until the loaf is braided. Press the strips together at the other end of the loaf.
5. Spray the cookie sheet lightly with vegetable oil cooking spray. Place the braided loaf on it and cover with a kitchen towel dusted lightly with flour. Place in a draft-free place (such as a microwave) to rise for 45 minutes.
6. While the bread rises, combine the brown sugar, white sugar, and cinnamon in a small bowl. Mix well.
7. Crack the egg over a small bowl and plop the egg into the center of the egg separator. Hold the separator over the bowl. The egg white will separate from the yolk and go into the bowl. Discard the yolk. Add the water and stir with the fork. Set aside.
8. When the bread has risen for 45 minutes, use the pastry brush to brush it with the egg white mixture, then sprinkle it evenly with the sugar-cinnamon mixture.
9. Bake bread for about 35 minutes or until the bread is golden brown.
10. Using oven mitts, remove the cookie sheet from the oven and let the bread cool for 10 minutes. Serve the bread warm.

Tropical Chicken Kabobs

***Kabobs** are small pieces of meat, poultry, seafood, or vegetables cooked on a skewer (a metal or bamboo stick with one pointed end). Kabobs are usually broiled. (Broiling is a good cooking method because it doesn't add any fat, as frying does.) For greater flavor, brush the kabobs with the sauce several times during cooking. This recipe uses olive oil, which is made from olives and contains much fat, but is healthier for you than an animal fat, such as butter. Olive oil, as well as canola oil, helps lower the cholesterol level in your blood.*

Time
30 minutes to prepare
plus
10 minutes to cook

Tools
4 metal
or
bamboo skewers

paring knife

cutting board

small bowl

wire whip

broiler pan

pastry brush

oven mitts

Makes
4 kabobs

Ingredients

- 2 small onions
- 1 red pepper
- 2 green peppers
- 8 cherry tomatoes
- 1 pound boneless, skinless chicken breast
- 1 cup pineapple chunks, fresh or canned
- ¼ cup teriyaki sauce
- 1 tablespoon soy sauce
- 2 tablespoons honey
- 1 tablespoon olive oil
- vegetable oil cooking spray

Teriyaki is a Japanese dish in which meat, poultry, seafood, or vegetables are marinated in wine and sweetened soy sauce. The meat is then broiled or barbecued with the sauce.

Steps

1. If using bamboo skewers, soak the skewers for 1 hour in warm water.
2. Remove the papery outer skin of the onions. On the cutting board, use the paring knife to cut each onion in half. Lay each onion half cut-side down on the cutting board and cut in half again.
3. Wash the red and green peppers and tomatoes.
4. Cut each pepper in half. Remove and discard the seeds and ribs from inside the peppers. Cut each pepper half into 4 wedges of similar size.

5. Using the knife on a clean cutting board, cut the chicken into 1-inch pieces. Wash the cutting board in warm, soapy water.
6. To assemble the kabobs, put 1 chicken piece, 1 onion piece, 1 green pepper wedge, 1 red pepper wedge, 1 tomato, and 1 pineapple chunk onto a skewer. Repeat this pattern on the same skewer until it's full.
7. Repeat step 6 with the other 3 skewers.
8. Put the teriyaki sauce, soy sauce, honey, and olive oil in the small bowl and whisk together with the wire whip.
9. Preheat the broiler.
10. Spray the broiler pan with vegetable oil cooking spray and place the kabobs on the broiler pan.
11. With the pastry brush, brush the kabobs with the teriyaki mixture.
12. Place the kabobs about 6 inches from the heating element and broil for 5 minutes. Keep an eye on the kabobs at all times to make sure they do not overcook and burn!
13. Using oven mitts, slide the broiler pan out and turn the kabobs over. Brush again with the teriyaki mixture. Broil about 4 minutes more, watching carefully.
14. Remove and serve.

Honey-Raisin Pick-Me-Up Popcorn Snack

This is an easy, low-fat recipe that has lots of flavor. It is great as a snack or in your lunchbox.

Time
20 minutes
plus
5 minutes to cook

Tools
large bowl
large frying pan
wooden spoon
baking pan with 1½" sides
oven mitts

Makes
24 squares

Ingredients

10 cups popped popcorn
1½ cups sliced almonds
1 cup raisins
¼ cup margarine
⅔ cup honey
vegetable cooking spray

Steps

1. Preheat the oven to 350°F.
2. Put the popcorn in the large bowl. Add the almonds and raisins and mix well.
3. Melt the margarine in the frying pan over medium heat.
4. Once the margarine is melted, add the honey. Turn the burner off.
5. Pour the margarine-honey mixture over the popcorn and stir with the wooden spoon until the popcorn is thoroughly coated.
6. Spray the baking pan with vegetable cooking spray.
7. Pour the popcorn mixture onto the baking pan. Press it into the pan. If the mixture sticks to your hands too much, dampen your hands with cold water.
8. Bake 3 to 5 minutes to warm.
9. Using oven mitts, remove pan from oven. Cut the popcorn into 24 squares.

Meringue Shell Filled with Fresh Fruit and Frozen Yogurt

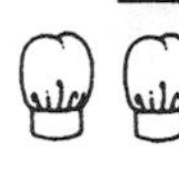

Time
30 minutes to prepare
plus
1½ hours to bake

Tools
cookie sheet
egg separator
2 medium bowls
handheld electric mixer
spatula
cookie sheet
oven mitts
paper towels
cutting board
paring knife
spoon

Makes
1 large meringue shell
(8 servings)

***Meringue** is a mixture of egg whites and sugar that is baked. It is a popular topping on pies, such as lemon meringue pie, but can also be baked as a pie shell. Once cooled, you can fill your meringue pie shell with a variety of foods to make a delicious dessert. This low-fat recipe uses three kinds of berries (any fruit can be used) and frozen yogurt as a filling.*

Ingredients

vegetable oil cooking spray
6 egg whites
⅛ teaspoon salt
1¾ cup sugar
1 teaspoon cornstarch
1 teaspoon vanilla extract
1 teaspoon vinegar
8 large strawberries
1 cup blueberries
1 cup raspberries
3 tablespoons sugar
4 cups frozen yogurt, your favorite flavor

Steps

1. Preheat the oven to 275°F.
2. Lightly spray the cookie sheet with vegetable oil cooking spray.
3. Crack 1 egg over a medium bowl and plop the egg into the center of the egg separator. Hold the separator over the bowl. The egg white will separate from the yolk and go into the bowl. Discard the yolk. Do the same with the remaining eggs.
4. Add the salt to the egg whites. Using the handheld electric mixer, beat the egg whites until soft peaks form.
5. Add 1¾ cups of sugar, 1 teaspoon at a time. Continue beating on a high speed until stiff peaks form when you lift the beater up.

●●●●●
Did you know that egg whites contain no fat or cholesterol? The egg yolk contains all of the fat and cholesterol and almost all of the calories of the whole egg.
●●●●●

6. Using the spatula, gently stir in the cornstarch, vanilla extract, and vinegar.
7. Mound the mixture on the cookie sheet. Form the mound into a large shell by making a depression in the center with the spatula. Make sure the mound is spread out.
8. Bake for 1½ hours until the shell is light pink in color. Turn off the heat. Leave the shell in the oven for 10 minutes while it starts to cool. Remove the cookie sheet with oven mitts.
9. While the shell is baking, look at strawberries, blueberries, and raspberries, and throw away any that have become moldy. Then wash the other berries and pat them dry with paper towels.
10. On the cutting board, slice the tops off the strawberries with the paring knife. Cut each strawberry into 4 pieces. Place into a medium bowl.
11. Add the blueberries and raspberries to the bowl with the strawberries. Add the 3 tablespoons of sugar and toss gently with a spoon.
12. Fill the cooled meringue shell with the fresh fruits and frozen yogurt and serve.

Cool-Down Watermelon Berry Drink

Time
5 minutes

Tools
cutting board

paring knife

electric blender

paper towels

Makes
2 servings

This is a refreshing drink to have when you need to cool down after exercising.

Ingredients

- 2 1-inch slices of watermelon
- 4 strawberries
- 1 cup raspberry-flavored seltzer
- 1 teaspoon vanilla syrup
- 1½ scoops raspberry sherbet
- 3 ice cubes

Steps

1. On the cutting board, use the paring knife to cut the watermelon into 1-inch cubes. Remove the seeds.
2. Put the watermelon into the blender. Cover and blend on medium for 30 seconds. Set aside.
3. Wash the strawberries and pat dry with paper towels. On the cutting board, cut the tops off the strawberries. Cut each strawberry in half.

To make this recipe quicker, buy seedless watermelons. Some seedless melons have tiny, soft, white seeds that are edible.

4. Put the strawberries, seltzer, vanilla syrup, sherbet, and ice cubes in the blender with the watermelon.
5. Cover and blend on medium speed until smooth.
6. Pour into glasses and serve.

CHAPTER 2

THE TRAVELING BLOOD SHOW

The heart, blood, and blood vessels make up the body's **circulatory system.** In the circulatory system, **blood** travels all around your body performing important jobs.

Blood travels over 100,000 miles through your blood vessels. When oxygen-rich blood leaves the heart, it travels in vessels called **arteries.** Arteries have muscles in their walls that push the blood along. Each artery branches, becoming smaller and smaller. The smallest arteries lead into another type of blood vessel, called **capillaries.** Capillaries have very thin walls and are so narrow that red blood cells must line up single file to travel through them. Capillaries join other capillaries, eventually forming another type of blood vessel called **veins.** Veins return blood to the heart.

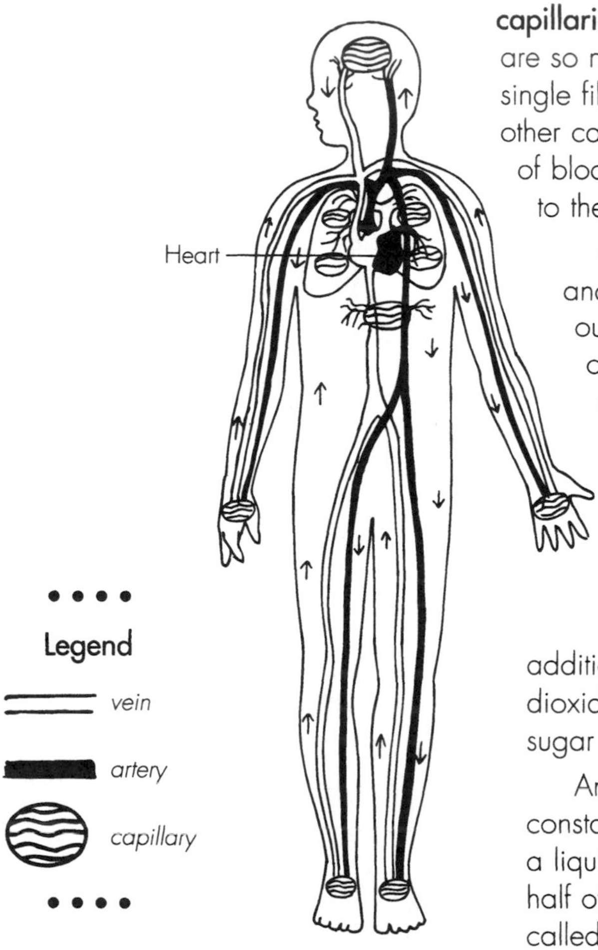

Heart

Legend

vein

artery

capillary

Blood picks up **oxygen** from the lungs and then goes to the heart to be pumped out to all the body's **cells.** The cells use oxygen to make energy. Cells produce **carbon dioxide,** a waste that needs to be taken out of the body. When blood delivers oxygen to the cells, it also picks up carbon dioxide. The blood then takes the carbon dioxide back to the lungs where it is pushed out when you exhale (breathe out). In addition to transporting oxygen and carbon dioxide, blood also transports nutrients such as sugar and vitamins.

An adult has about five quarts of blood constantly traveling around the body. Blood is a liquid that contains many substances. About half of your blood is a watery yellow liquid called **plasma.**

The rest of your blood contains three types of blood cells: red blood cells, white blood cells, and platelets. **Red blood cells** contain **iron,** a mineral that makes it possible for oxygen to be transported to the cells. We must eat some iron-rich foods every day to keep our red blood cells healthy. Iron-rich foods include meat, shellfish, dried beans, green leafy vegetables, and breads and cereals. Dried fruits are also a good source of iron.

White blood cells defend the body from intruders, such as germs. **Platelets,** as you will see in the activity, make it possible for blood to clot, or stop bleeding, when you get a cut.

Do the following activity to see how platelets help prevent bleeding.

ACTIVITY

WHAT STOPS BLEEDING FROM A CUT?

Purpose

To see how platelets stop bleeding.

Materials

1 manila file folder or 1 sheet (8½" × 11") posterboard
ruler
scissors
pencil
2 glasses
cotton ball
hole puncher
1 piece red and 1 piece white construction paper

Steps

1. From the file folder or posterboard, cut two 4-inch squares.

2. Fold each square in half. With a pencil, mark a notch about 1 inch long and ½-inch wide. Cut out the notch. Unfold each square and place one square on the top of each glass.

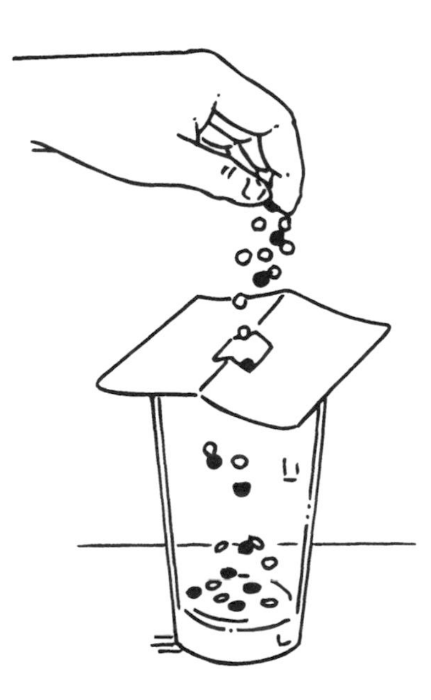

3. Pull a small piece of cotton from the cotton ball. Stretch it across the hole in the paper on one glass. Make sure a thin layer of cotton fibers covers the hole.
4. With the hole puncher, punch out 20 red circles and 20 white circles from the construction paper.
5. Take 10 red and 10 white circles in your hand. Hold them about 2 inches above the hole in the paper on the glass without the cotton. Drop them over the hole.
6. Repeat step 5, dropping the circles over the glass with the cotton.

What Happened?

The circles, which represent red and white blood cells, could not get through the hole covered with cotton. The hole in the paper represents a cut in the skin. Without platelets, red and white blood cells would flow out the opening. This is what happened with the first glass. Platelets do two things to prevent bleeding. First, they clump together to trap other cells. Second, platelets have a role in creating **fibrin,** which looks and acts much like the cotton threads and helps in clotting blood. When the clot dries and hardens on the surface of your skin, it is called a **scab.**

Try one of these high-iron recipes to keep your blood healthy.

Individual Tex-Mex Meatloaves

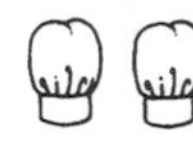

Time
20 minutes to prepare
plus
30 minutes to bake

Tools
cutting board
paring knife
1-gallon resealable plastic bag
rolling pin
medium bowl
wooden spoon
cookie sheet
oven mitts

Makes
6 individual meatloaves

Tex-Mex cooking combines the influences of Texas and Mexico. This recipe uses two staples of Mexican cooking: tortilla chips and salsa. Salsa is a popular Mexican sauce made from tomatoes, onions, chili peppers, garlic, and sometimes other ingredients. The Tex-Mex flavors give the classic meatloaf dish a new zip, and the lean ground beef gives you lots of iron.

Ingredients

1 small onion
12 tortilla chips
1½ pounds lean ground beef or poultry
¾ cup salsa
1 egg
1 teaspoon ground cumin
½ teaspoon chili powder
¼ teaspoon salt
vegetable oil cooking spray
6 tablespoons salsa
½ cup shredded Monterey Jack cheese

Tortillas are thin, flat pancakes eaten as bread at most Mexican meals. This recipe uses tortilla chips, which are simply small tortilla pieces that have been baked or fried.

Steps

1. Preheat the oven to 375°F.
2. Remove the papery outer skin of the onion. On the cutting board, use the paring knife to cut the onion in half. Lay each onion half cut-side down on the cutting board and chop.

3. Place 6 tortilla chips in the plastic bag. Press the air out of the bag and seal. With the rolling pin, crush the tortilla chips, using a back-and-forth motion, until they are finely crushed. Continue with the rest of the chips until you have ½ cup.
4. In the medium bowl, mix the chopped onion, crushed tortilla chips, ground beef, ¾ cup salsa, egg, cumin, chili powder, and salt. Blend the mixture with a wooden spoon until well mixed.
5. Spray the cookie sheet with vegetable oil cooking spray.
6. Divide the mixture into 6 equal portions. Shape each to form round loaves on the cookie sheet.
7. Bake for 25 minutes. Using oven mitts, remove the cookie sheet from the oven. Top each loaf with 1 tablespoon salsa and sprinkle with cheese. Return to the oven for 5 minutes to melt the cheese.
8. Remove from the oven and serve.

One-Pot Creamy Navy Bean and Potato Soup

Time
40 minutes to prepare
plus
55 minutes to cook

Tools
cutting board
paring knife
vegetable peeler
large pot with lid
wooden spoon
can opener

Makes
8 1½-cup servings

Dried beans, such as navy beans, are good sources of iron and many other nutrients. This is a hearty soup for lunch or supper on a cold winter day.

Ingredients

- 6 scallions
- 3 carrots
- 3 celery stalks
- 2 medium red potatoes
- ½ head small cabbage
- 3 tablespoons vegetable oil
- 2 15-ounce cans navy beans
- 1 teaspoon dried oregano
- ½ teaspoon dried marjoram
- ¼ teaspoon pepper
- 2 cups vegetable broth
- 2 cups chicken broth
- 2 cups skim or low-fat milk
- fresh or dried parsley for garnish

Steps

1. Wash and dry the scallions, carrots, celery, potatoes, and cabbage.
2. On the cutting board, use the paring knife to cut the root end and the green stems off the scallions. Discard these and cut the remaining white part of the scallions into ¼-inch slices.
3. Peel the carrots with the vegetable peeler. Cut the peeled carrots into ¼-inch slices.
4. Cut off and discard the ends of the celery stalks. Slice each stalk lengthwise into 2 strips, then chop them into small pieces.
5. Peel the potatoes. Cut the potatoes in half. Lay the potatoes cut-side down on the cutting board and slice them into ¼-inch slices. Cut each slice into small cubes.

6. Lay the cabbage head on the cutting board cut-side down. Slice the cabbage into ¼-inch strips.
7. Put the oil in the bottom of the large pot. Put the pot on a burner set to medium heat.
8. Add the scallions, carrots, and celery to the pot. Sauté until tender, about 5 minutes, stirring with the wooden spoon.
9. Open the cans of navy beans. Put the beans and their liquid into the pot.
10. Add the potatoes, cabbage, oregano, marjoram, and pepper. Cover the pot and steam the vegetables for 10 minutes. Check every 2 to 3 minutes to make sure there is some liquid at the bottom of the pot. If the bottom is dry, add ½ cup water.
11. Add the vegetable and chicken broths. Cover again and simmer for 30 minutes.
12. Add the milk and cook the soup for 10 more minutes.
13. Ladle the soup into bowls. Sprinkle with parsley.

Dried Fruit and Nut Quick Energy Mix

Time
15 minutes

Tools
cutting board

paring knife

medium bowl

wooden spoon

resealable plastic sandwich bags

Makes
5 cups or
20 ¼-cup servings

Dried fruits are full of iron. In only 15 minutes, you can make this great mix that you can pack in your lunchbox, in your bike bag, or in your knapsack. It will give you iron and energy wherever you go!

Ingredients

1 cup dried apples
1 cup dried apricots
1 cup dried banana chips
1 cup sunflower seeds
½ cup dry roasted peanuts
½ cup raisins

Steps

1. On the cutting board, use the paring knife to cut the apple into bite-size pieces.

2. Cut the apricots into ¼-inch strips.
3. In the bowl, use the wooden spoon to mix together the apple pieces, apricot strips, banana chips, sunflower seeds, peanuts, and raisins. Mix well.
4. Put the dried fruit mix into the resealable plastic bags.

Dried fruit has had at least half of its water content removed. This is why it is chewy to eat and very sweet.

Easy Cheese and Spinach Rice

Time
30 minutes

Tools
3-quart saucepan with lid

wooden spoon

Makes
4 servings

Popeye didn't get his energy from eating chips and dip! He ate lots of spinach, which is packed with many nutrients, including iron.

Ingredients

- 2 cups water
- 2 chicken bouillon cubes
- 1 10½-ounce package frozen chopped spinach
- 1 cup brown or white rice
- ½ cup grated sharp cheddar cheese

Steps

1. In the 3-quart saucepan, bring the water, bouillon cubes, and spinach to a boil.
2. Add the rice to the pot. Lower the heat to a simmer and cover the pot. Cook for as long as the rice package instructions state.
3. Take the pot off the heat. Let it sit, covered, for 5 minutes.
4. Stir the rice and spinach with the wooden spoon. Add the cheese. Stir until the cheese melts and the mixture is well blended. Serve immediately.

CHAPTER 3 MUSCULAR MOTIONS

Almost half your body weight is **muscles**! Muscles are controlled by signals from your brain. You depend on the more than 600 muscles in your body for motion of any type, from closing your eyes to running a race. Your biggest muscles are in your thighs and buttocks. Muscles allow you to kick a soccer ball, write notes, use a computer, and do almost everything.

You have three different kinds of muscles. **Skeletal muscles,** which are usually attached to bones, pull on your bones to make them move. When muscles pull, they get shorter and thicker. Since muscles cannot push, they often work in pairs. For example, the biceps muscle pulls to bend the elbow. The triceps muscle then pulls the arm straight again.

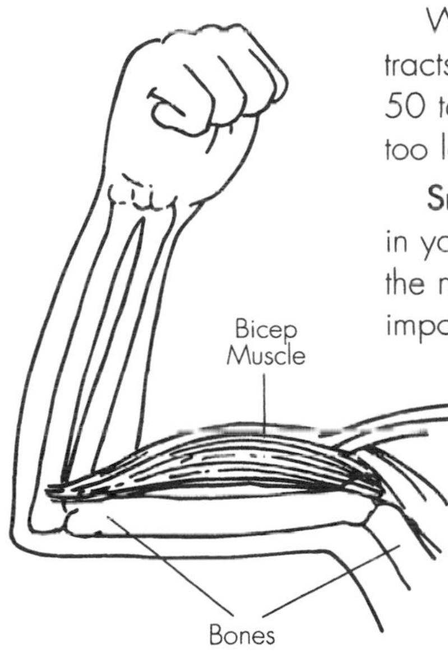

When you bend your elbow, it feels as if the muscle contracts once. In fact, it's contracting and relaxing anywhere from 50 to 150 times during that moment. If your muscles contract for too long, you feel a cramp.

Smooth muscles are found in the walls of blood vessels and in your stomach and other internal organs. You cannot control the movement of smooth muscles. These muscles perform many important jobs, such as moving food from your mouth to your stomach and through the intestines. **Cardiac muscle** is found only in the heart. It is a specialized type of muscle that contracts every second or so, yet never tires.

The building block of muscle is **protein,** a nutrient. About one-sixth of your body's weight is protein. Protein in your diet is used to repair and rebuild muscle cells. Meat, poultry, fish, and eggs are high-protein foods. Milk and dairy products and dried beans and peas also supply protein.

Muscles need to be used regularly to stay healthy. The muscles you use repeatedly will become larger, firmer, and stronger. Muscles that are used occasionally are smaller and weaker. Do the following activity to learn about how to warm up your muscles before a game or workout.

ACTIVITY

WHY IS IT A GOOD IDEA TO WARM UP BEFORE SPORTS?

Purpose

To understand the benefits of warm-up exercises.

Materials

Wear loose-fitting clothes and sneakers.

Steps

1. Before doing a sports activity, such as soccer, perform the following warm-up exercises.
   - Upper Body Twists: Stand up straight with your feet about 2 inches apart. Put your hands on your hips. Gently twist from your waist to your right and then to your left. Repeat 5 times.
   - Shoulder Rolls: In same position, with hands on hips, rotate your shoulders forward 5 times, then backward 5 times.
   - Whole Body Stretch: Lie down on the floor on your back. Put your hands over your head and stretch your whole body. Keep your lower back flat on the floor while you stretch. Repeat 5 times.

- Knee Push-Ups: Roll over onto your stomach. Push up from your knees. Keep your body straight from your knees to your shoulders. Repeat 5 times.
- Jog slowly in place for 2 minutes.

2. On another day, jump right into a sports activity without doing any warm-ups.

What Happened?

The exercises you did are designed to get your body ready for exercise. They are called "warm-ups" because they raise muscle temperature, which makes muscles easier to stretch and less likely to be hurt during your game or workout. Warm-up exercises also slowly raise your heart rate to where it will be during your game or workout. When you didn't perform the exercises, it probably took you a little longer to get up to your normal level of performance.

Check out these protein-booster recipes to keep your muscles healthy and happy.

Hi-Pro Scrambled Eggs with Heart-Shaped Toast Cutouts

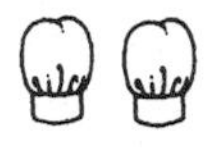

Time
15 minutes

Tools
small bowl

wire whip

10-inch nonstick frying pan with cover

wooden spoon

spatula

toaster

4-inch heart-shaped cookie cutter

sandwich spreader

Makes
2 brunch servings

Eggs are a great way to get high-quality protein.

This is a great recipe to make on Mother's Day or Father's Day to remind someone special that you care! It's quick to make but leaves a lasting impression.

Ingredients

4 large eggs

4 tablespoons skim or low-fat milk

¼ teaspoon pepper

vegetable oil cooking spray

4 slices whole wheat bread

¼ cup fruit preserves, any flavor

Steps

1. Break the eggs, one at a time, into the small bowl.
2. Add the milk and pepper to the bowl, and whisk with the wire whip until the mixture is foamy.
3. Spray the frying pan with vegetable oil cooking spray.
4. Add the egg mixture to the pan and place over medium heat.
5. Lightly stir the egg mixture with the wooden spoon until the eggs begin to set or become firm. Allow the eggs to cook for 2 minutes longer.
6. With the spatula, turn the eggs over and cook on the other side for about 2 to 3 minutes. The eggs should be light yellow in color and cooked all the way through. Remove the pan from the burner and cover.
7. Put the whole wheat bread in the toaster and toast on a light setting.

8. Cut each slice of toast with the heart-shaped cookie cutter. With the sandwich spreader, spread the toast hearts with fruit preserves.
9. Divide the eggs evenly onto two serving plates. Serve with 2 toast hearts per person.

After-the-Workout Tuna Veggie Melt

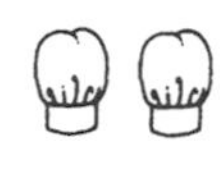

Time
30 minutes

Tools
can opener
medium bowl
paper towels
cutting board
paring knife
vegetable peeler
wooden spoon
toaster
cookie sheet
oven mitts

Makes
4 servings

Tuna fish is packed in cans in either water or oil. Water-packed tuna contains less fat and fewer calories than oil-packed.

This is a great snack to make after you've exercised. The tuna is high in protein, and the cheese adds protein as well.

Ingredients

- 1 6½-ounce can tuna fish, packed in water
- 1 scallion
- 1 stalk celery
- 1 small carrot
- 3 tablespoons low-fat mayonnaise
- ¼ teaspoon pepper
- 2 whole wheat English muffins
- vegetable oil cooking spray
- 4 slices American cheese

Steps

1. Open the tuna fish can and drain off the liquid. Put the tuna fish in the bowl.
2. Wash and dry the scallion, celery stalk, and carrot.
3. On the cutting board, use the paring knife to cut the root end and green stem off the scallion. Discard these and slice the remaining white section into ¼-inch pieces and chop.
4. Cut the ends off of the celery stalk and discard them. Slice the celery lengthwise into two strips, then cut into small pieces.
5. Peel the carrot with the vegetable peeler. Cut the peeled carrot into ¼-inch slices.
6. Mix the scallions, celery, and carrot with the tuna fish, using the wooden spoon. Add the mayonnaise and pepper and stir well.
7. Preheat the broiler. Split open each English muffin to get 4 muffin halves. Lightly toast the muffins in the toaster.

8. Coat the cookie sheet with vegetable oil cooking spray. Put the muffin halves on the cookie sheet.
9. Divide the tuna fish mixture into 4 equal portions and heap onto the muffin halves. Top each muffin with a slice of cheese.
10. Place the cookie sheet under the broiler until the cheese is melted and begins to bubble, about 1 minute. Keep your eye on the sandwiches and don't let the cheese brown. Use oven mitts to take the cookie sheet out of the oven.
11. Let muffins cool for 2 to 3 minutes before serving.

Crunchy Chicken Fingers

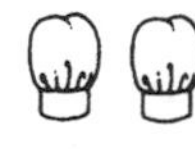

Time
10 minutes to prepare
plus
10 to 12 minutes to cook

Tools
cookie sheet

1-gallon resealable plastic bag

2 medium bowls

wire whip

cutting board

paring knife

fork

oven mitts

Makes
6 servings

These chicken fingers get their crunch from wheat germ. Wheat germ is a part of the wheat grain. Both chicken and eggs are high in protein.

Ingredients

vegetable oil cooking spray
1 cup all-purpose flour
¼ teaspoon black pepper
¼ teaspoon salt
2 eggs
¼ cup skim or low-fat milk
1 cup toasted wheat germ
4 skinless, boneless chicken breast halves

Steps

1. Preheat the oven to 400°F.
2. Spray the cookie sheet with vegetable oil cooking spray.
3. Place the flour, black pepper, and salt in the plastic bag. Seal the bag and shake it to mix the ingredients well. Set aside.
4. Whisk the eggs and milk together in one of the bowls, using the wire whip.
5. Place the wheat germ in the other bowl.
6. On the cutting board, use the paring knife to cut the chicken into strips, about 4 inches long by ½-inch wide.
7. Put the chicken fingers into the plastic bag with the flour mixture. Seal the bag and shake. When all the pieces are coated with flour, remove the chicken from the bag.
8. Using the fork, dip the chicken strips, two at a time, into the egg mixture, then into the wheat germ.

9. Place the chicken fingers in a single layer on the cookie sheet.
10. Bake for 10 to 12 minutes, or until lightly golden brown. Remove the cookie sheet from the oven using oven mitts.
11. Serve with your favorite sauce, if desired.

Tapioca Pudding and Tri-Berry Fruit Parfait

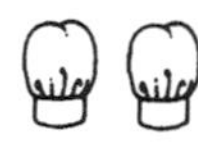

Time
30 minutes to prepare
plus
2 hours to chill

Tools
3-quart saucepan
wooden spoon
egg separator
2 medium bowls
handheld electric mixer
spatula
paper towels
cutting board
paring knife
8 parfait glasses

Makes
8 parfaits

Tapioca comes from a plant and is used to thicken various dishes. When cooked, the tiny particles become clear.

For a very attractive and fancy dessert, try this recipe. It uses three types of berries--blueberries, raspberries, and strawberries—but you can use any fruit you like. Just be sure it's colorful and can be served in bite-size pieces. The milk and eggs in this recipe provide lots of protein.

Ingredients

½ cup sugar
¼ cup quick-cooking tapioca
¼ teaspoon salt
4 cups skim or low-fat milk
3 eggs
1½ teaspoons vanilla extract
½ cup light whipping cream
2 cups blueberries
1 cup raspberries
1 cup strawberries
2 tablespoons sugar

Steps

1. Put the ½ cup of sugar, tapioca, and salt in the saucepan, and stir well with the wooden spoon to combine.
2. Stir in the milk and continue to mix until the sugar is dissolved. Let the mixture sit for 5 minutes.
3. Meanwhile, one at a time, crack each egg over a bowl and plop the egg into the center of an egg separator. Hold the separator over the bowl. The egg white will separate from the yolk and go into the bowl. Add the egg yolks to the milk mixture and stir well. Discard the egg whites.
4. Heat the milk mixture over a medium heat, stirring constantly, until the mixture begins to boil. Once boiling, remove from the heat. Stir in the vanilla extract.

5. Put the cream in a clean bowl and beat with the electric mixer until stiff peaks form when you lift the beater up. This takes about 2 to 3 minutes. Do not over beat!
6. With the spatula, gently fold the milk mixture into the bowl with the whipped cream, using an over-and-under motion.
7. Chill the mixture in the refrigerator for 2 hours or until the pudding is thick and creamy.
8. Look through the blueberries, raspberries, and strawberries, and discard any that have become moldy. Then wash the rest of the berries and pat them dry with paper towels.
9. On the cutting board, use the paring knife to slice off the top of the strawberries. With cut-side down on the cutting board, slice each strawberry into ¼-inch slices.
10. In a medium bowl, mix together the blueberries, raspberries, and strawberries. Sprinkle with the 2 tablespoons of sugar and toss gently.
11. To assemble, place 2 tablespoons of the fruit mixture in the bottom of a parfait glass. Spoon about ¼ cup of the tapioca pudding over the fruit. Repeat until the glass is filled to the top. Fill the remaining glasses the same way and chill in the refrigerator.

Pick-a-Flavor Power Boost Shake

Time
5 minutes

Tools
electric blender

Makes
2 servings

For a boost of protein—from the milk and yogurt—pick your favorite flavor and go to work making a delicious shake!

Ingredients

Vanilla Shake:

1½ cups skim or low-fat milk
2 tablespoons vanilla syrup
1 cup vanilla frozen yogurt
4 ice cubes

Chocolate Shake:

1½ cups skim or low-fat milk
2 tablespoons chocolate syrup
1 cup chocolate frozen yogurt
4 ice cubes

Banana Shake:

1½ cups skim or low-fat milk
1 ripe banana
1 cup vanilla frozen yogurt
4 ice cubes

Steps

1. Put all the ingredients for the shake flavor you've chosen, except the ice cubes, into the blender.
2. Cover and blend on high speed until smooth.
3. Add the ice cubes. Blend on high again until the ice is crushed.
4. Pour into glasses and serve.

CHAPTER 4 LONG, STRONG BONES!

Your body has more than 200 bones! **Bones** are the hard, stiff parts of your body that make up your skeleton. Your skeleton supports your body, just like the frame of a house supports its roof and walls. Bones also protect the organs in your body from getting hurt. And you need bones in order to walk, run, or move in any way. Bones also make something you can't live without: red blood cells and white blood cells (as discussed in chapter 2).

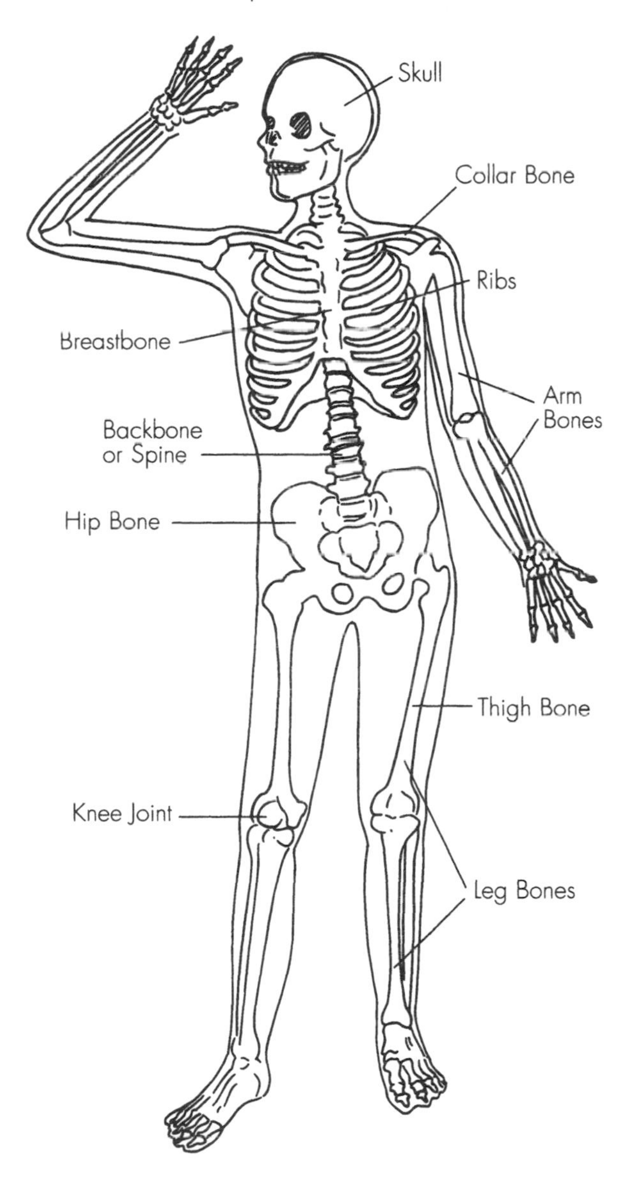

The illustration shows many of the major bones in your body. All of your bones are light but very strong. Bones have different shapes depending on what they do. Your **backbone,** or **spine,** provides the central support for your body. Your spine is made of 26 bones called **vertebrae.**

Bones cannot bend without **joints.** Joints are the places where your bones meet, such as your knee. Your knee lets you move your lower leg back and forth. Strong structures called **ligaments** join bones together in joints and allow bones to move.

Although they seem to be as lifeless as rocks, your bones are growing and will continue to grow until you are at least 30 years old. In order to have the strongest bones possible, it is important to get lots of **calcium,** a mineral found in many foods. Calcium-rich foods include milk and milk products, such as cheese, yogurt, and ice cream; as well as tofu (when made with calcium salts); and canned sardines or salmon (with the bones). Collard greens, okra, broccoli, and oranges also supply some calcium.

To make a drawing of the bones in your own body, try the following activity.

ACTIVITY

MY HIP BONE'S CONNECTED TO WHICH BONE?

Purpose

To identify bones in your skeleton.

Materials

a piece of paper large enough to draw your outline on

colored markers

helper

Steps

1. Put the piece of paper on the floor. Lie down on top of the paper.
2. Ask your helper to draw a line around your entire body.
3. Now, use the drawing in this book to draw the following bones in the appropriate places in your body outline: skull, breastbone, ribs, collar bone, arm bones, leg bones including thigh bone, hip bone, and backbone.
4. Circle the knee joint, shoulder joint, and elbow joint.

What Happened?

You've drawn your skeleton, including important bones and joints.

Now, to keep those bones strong and healthy, try your hand at preparing these delicious high-calcium recipes.

Wake-Me-Up Sunshine Salad

This salad could be served at any time of day, from morning to evening. The cottage cheese is full of calcium, and the oranges have a little as well. Have fun using the orange segments to make the sun's rays.

Time
15 minutes

Tools
knife

can opener

ice cream scoop
or
spoon

Makes
2 servings

Ingredients

1 orange

1 8-ounce can of pineapple rings, packed in juice

4 lettuce leaves

1 cup low-fat (1%) cottage cheese

2 maraschino cherries

Steps

1. Using a knife, make a small X on the top of the orange. Peel and section the orange.
2. Open the can of pineapple rings. Drain the liquid.
3. Place 2 washed lettuce leaves on each plate.
4. Place 2 pineapple rings on top of the lettuce on each plate.
5. Place 1 scoop of cottage cheese on top of the pineapple rings.
6. Place the orange segments around the cottage cheese on each plate to make the sun's rays.
7. Decorate the top of each salad with a cherry.

Cottage cheese was made in home kitchens all over Europe for centuries. It is called "cottage" cheese because farmers made it in their own cottages.

Garden Grilled Cheese Sandwich

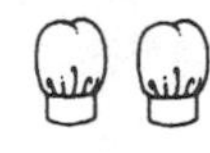

Time
15 minutes

Tools
paper towels
paring knife
cutting board
table knife
large nonstick frying pan
spatula

Makes
3 sandwiches

If grilled cheese is starting to get a little boring, try putting a little flavor and crunch into it with this recipe. The cheese is a good source of calcium.

Ingredients

1 cucumber
1 tomato
6 slices American cheese
6 slices whole wheat bread
3 tablespoons low-fat mayonnaise
vegetable oil cooking spray

Steps

1. Wash the cucumber and tomato and dry with paper towels.

2. Using the paring knife on the cutting board, slice the cucumber and tomato into ¼-inch slices. Set aside.

3. Place two slices of cheese on a slice of bread. Top with 4 slices of cucumber and 1 slice of tomato. Finish the sandwich by topping it with another piece of bread. Repeat this step to make two more sandwiches.

4. With a table knife, spread the outside of each slice of bread with mayonnaise. Set aside on the cutting board.

5. Spray the frying pan with vegetable oil cooking spray.

6. Place the sandwiches in the frying pan and cook over medium heat. Cook on one side for about 3 minutes, or until lightly browned.
7. Turn the sandwiches over with the spatula. Cook for 2 or 3 more minutes until the cheese is melted and the bread is golden brown.

Bodacious Bok Choy and Beef

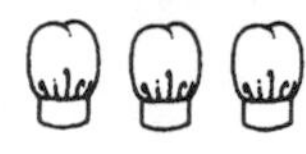

Time
35 minutes

Tools
paring knife
cutting board
large bowl
paper towels
2 small bowls
small spoon
wok or heavy frying pan with lid
slotted spoon
medium bowl

Makes
6 servings

Stir-frying is cooking bite-size foods over medium-high heat in a small amount of oil. The foods are moved constantly around the pan so they cook evenly and quickly over the high heat.

***Bok choy** is a kind of Chinese cabbage that is popular in Oriental dishes. It has long, white stalks like celery and large, deep green leaves. It has a sweet and mild flavor, and it's loaded with calcium.*

Ingredients

- 1 large head of bok choy
- 2 stalks celery
- 4 scallions
- 2 cloves garlic
- 1 pound sirloin steak
- 1 cup beef broth
- 2 tablespoons soy sauce
- 2 tablespoons cornstarch
- 2 tablespoons cold water
- 2 tablespoons peanut oil
- 3 cups cooked brown or white rice

Steps

1. On the cutting board, use the paring knife to cut off the base of the bok choy. Pull the stalks apart. Throw out any ragged or discolored leaves. Soak the bok choy in a large bowl of cold water to remove any sand or dirt. Set aside.
2. Wash the celery and scallions and dry with paper towels.
3. Using the paring knife and cutting board, cut off and discard the leaves and ends of the celery. Then cut off and discard the roots and wilted leaf ends of the scallions.
4. Slice the celery diagonally. Cut the scallions into ¼-inch slices.
5. Peel the outer covering of the garlic. Cut the garlic into very small pieces.
6. Take the bok choy out of the water and dry with paper towels.

7. Slice the bok choy into 1-inch pieces until you have 4 cups.
8. Wash the paring knife and cutting board.
9. Using the paring knife and cutting board, cut the sirloin steak into 1-inch-long strips. Cut each strip into 1-inch cubes.
10. In a small bowl, mix together the beef broth and soy sauce.
11. In another small bowl, mix the cornstarch and cold water together with the small spoon until it is smooth. Set aside.
12. Heat the peanut oil in the wok or frying pan over medium heat. Add the beef and stir-fry for 3 minutes using the slotted spoon. Remove the beef from the wok and place in the medium bowl.
13. Add the garlic, celery, scallions, and bok choy to the wok. Stir-fry for about 3 minutes until the vegetables are crisp.
14. Add the beef broth mixture and return the beef cubes to the wok. Bring to a boil by covering for about 2 minutes.
15. Add the cornstarch and water slowly to the stir-fry, stirring constantly. Cook until the liquid is thickened and the beef and vegetables are coated with a thin glaze.
16. Serve stir-fry over rice.

Creamy, Dreamy Yogurt Orange-Banana Frozen Pops

Time
10 minutes
plus
2 hours to freeze

Tools
can opener

electric blender

8 3-ounce paper cups and wooden sticks,
or
8 plastic ice-pop molds

aluminum foil

Makes
8 ice pops

Make your own frozen treats with this simple recipe. If you don't have ice-pop molds, you can use paper cups and wooden sticks. Most of the calcium in this recipe comes from the yogurt, but oranges have some, too.

Ingredients

- ¼ cup mandarin orange pieces
- ½ cup orange juice concentrate, thawed
- 1¾ cups vanilla yogurt
- 1 small ripe banana

Steps

1. Open the can of mandarin oranges. Drain out the liquid. Measure ¼ cup in a measuring cup.
2. Put the mandarin orange pieces, orange juice concentrate, vanilla yogurt, and banana in the blender container. Blend on medium speed until the mixture is smooth.
3. Pour the mixture into 3-ounce paper cups or plastic molds. If using paper cups, cover each cup with a small piece of aluminum foil.
4. Put the cups or molds into the freezer and freeze until the mixture is thick and slushy, about 30 to 40 minutes.
5. Remove the cups from the freezer. Insert a wooden stick through the foil covering each cup and push the stick to the bottom of the cup. If using plastic molds, insert plastic sticks.

6. Return the cups to the freezer and freeze until the juice is completely hard, about 2 hours.
7. To eat, hold onto the stick and peel off the paper cup. If using molds, hold the plastic mold under warm tap water until the pop loosens, about 30 to 60 seconds.

CHAPTER 5 "LOOK, MOM, NO CAVITIES!"

The hardest substance in your body is found in your mouth. It is called **enamel** and it forms a protective surface over each of your teeth. Look in the mirror at your teeth. The part of each tooth that you can see is called the **crown.** The enamel protects the crown. Under the enamel, the tooth is made mostly of dentin. **Dentin** is like bone, but harder. Some blood vessels and nerves are also in your teeth.

You are born with all the teeth you will ever have. Between the time when you were 6 months to 3 years old, 20 baby teeth (also called **deciduous** or **milk teeth**) pushed out of your gums. Starting at about 6 years of age, the milk teeth started to fall out and adult teeth pushed through the gums. By age 20, most people have all of their adult teeth—32 in all.

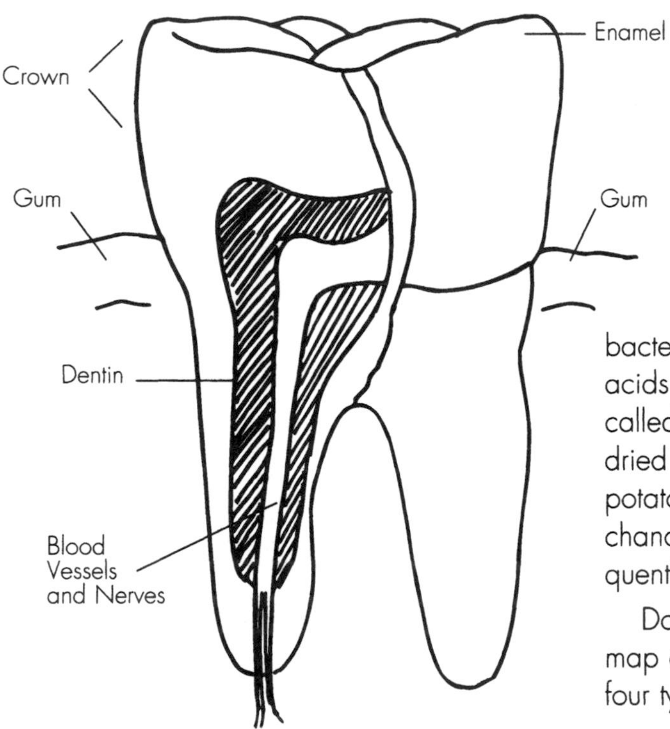

Germs known as **bacteria** live in your mouth. Teeth are good places for bacteria to grow. Bacteria love to eat certain foods, such as sweets and starchy foods. When these foods are in your mouth, the bacteria eat them and produce acids. The acids eventually cause holes in your teeth, called **cavities** or **caries.** Foods such as dried fruits, breads, cereals, crackers, potato chips, and sweets increase chances of dental caries when eaten frequently, especially between meals.

Do the following activity to make a map of your teeth and learn about the four types of teeth you have.

HOW MANY TEETH DO I HAVE?

ACTIVITY

Purpose

To count how many teeth you have and identify different types of teeth.

Materials

An apple or cheese wedge

Steps

1. Carefully bite into an apple or cheese wedge so that all your teeth leave a mark on it.
2. Look at the wedge to see the marks left by your teeth.
3. Count up the number of teeth that bit into the wedge.

What Happened?

You have made a map of your teeth. You should have between 20 and 32 teeth. Chances are some of your teeth are baby teeth and some are adult teeth.

Look at the kind of mark each tooth left. The teeth at the front of your mouth are called **incisors.** Incisors are shaped like knives and help cut and slice food. Just behind the incisors are teeth called **canines.** Canines are shaped like cones and help spear and tear food. Located behind the canines are the **premolars** and **molars.** The tops of these teeth are ideal for crushing and grinding food.

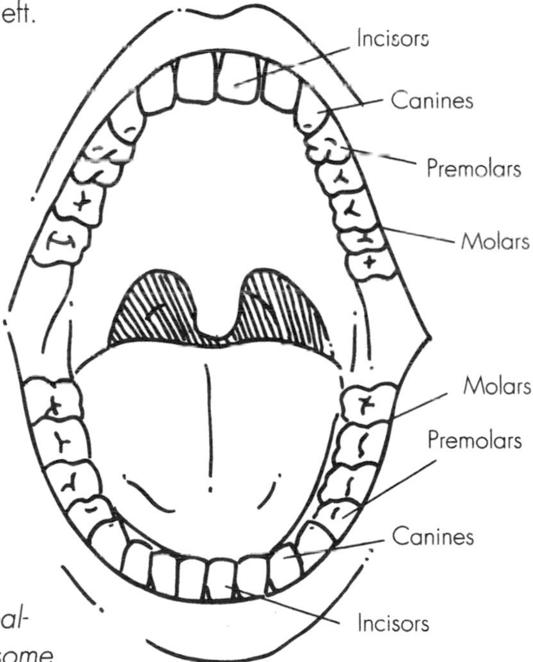

Foods that do not seem to cause cavities include some vegetables, meat and poultry, fish, cheeses, and nuts. Foods such as apples help clean your teeth. Remember to brush and floss your teeth often, try to limit sweets to meal-time, see your dentist regularly, and try some of the following recipes that don't encourage tooth decay.

Salsa Chicken

Time
10 minutes to prepare
plus
40 minutes to bake

Tools
baking pan

spoon

aluminum foil

oven mitts

Makes
4 servings

This is an easy way to spice up chicken and make it taste great. Salsa and Parmesan cheese add just the right flavors.

Ingredients

vegetable oil cooking spray

4 skinless, boneless chicken breast halves

1 cup salsa

¼ cup grated Parmesan cheese

Steps

1. Preheat the oven to 350°F.
2. Spray the baking pan with vegetable oil cooking spray.
3. Place the chicken breast halves in a single layer in the baking pan.
4. Spoon the salsa evenly over the chicken.
5. Sprinkle the Parmesan cheese evenly over the salsa.
6. Cover the pan with aluminum foil.
7. Bake for 30 minutes. Using oven mitts, remove the foil covering and bake 10 more minutes.

Veggie Nibbles

If vegetables still aren't your favorites, try this recipe. Breading and baking the vegetables gives them a nice taste and texture.

Ingredients

vegetable oil cooking spray
1 cup cauliflower or broccoli florets
2 medium carrots
1 green, red, or yellow bell pepper
1 egg
2 teaspoons water
½ cup all-purpose flour
¼ teaspoon salt
3 tablespoons margarine
¼ cup grated Parmesan cheese

Steps

1. Preheat the oven to 350°F.
2. Spray the baking pan with vegetable oil cooking spray.
3. Place the cauliflower or broccoli florets in the colander and wash.
4. Wash the carrots and pepper. Pat dry with paper towels.
5. Peel the carrots. Using the paring knife and cutting board, cut off the top and bottom of each carrot and discard. Cut the carrots into ¼-inch slices.
6. Cut the pepper in half. Remove and discard the ribs and seeds. Cut the pepper into ½-inch-wide strips.
7. In one shallow bowl, beat the egg and water together with a fork. Mix the flour and salt in the other shallow bowl.
8. Place 5 vegetable pieces at a time into the egg mixture. One at a time, remove the vegetable pieces with the slotted spoon and roll into the flour mixture to coat. Place in baking pan. Repeat with rest of vegetables.

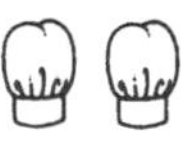

Time
30 minutes to prepare
plus
12 minutes to bake

Tools
13 × 9 × 2-inch baking pan
colander
paper towels
vegetable peeler
paring knife
cutting board
2 shallow bowls
fork
slotted spoon
small saucepan
oven mitts
spatula

Makes
5 half-cup servings

You can substitute your own favorite vegetables for the ones in this recipe if you like. Simply cut into bite-size pieces.

9. Melt the margarine in the saucepan over medium heat. Pour melted margarine over each vegetable piece in the baking pan.
10. Bake uncovered. After 5 minutes, put on your oven mitts and use a spatula to turn the vegetables over.
11. Bake 5 to 7 minutes more until the coating on the vegetables is golden brown.
12. Using oven mitts, remove the pan from the oven. Sprinkle the vegetables with Parmesan cheese.

Swiss Cheese Salad

Cheese and vegetables are tooth-friendly, so try them together in this recipe!

Ingredients

- ½ head iceberg lettuce
- ½ head red-tipped leaf lettuce
- 1 celery stalk
- 1 medium tomato
- ½ pound Swiss cheese (in one piece, not slices)
- ¾ cup your favorite fat-free salad dressing

Steps

1. Wash both heads of lettuce and pat dry with paper towels.
2. Using your hands, tear the lettuce into bite-size pieces. Throw out any pieces that are bruised or brown. Place the lettuce into the salad bowl.
3. Using the paring knife on the cutting board, cut off and discard the leaves and ends of the celery stalk. Cut the celery into thin slices and place in the salad bowl.
4. Wash and dry the tomato. Cut the tomato in half. Cut 6 tomato chunks from each tomato half. Add to the salad bowl.
5. Cut the Swiss cheese into bite-size chunks and add to the salad bowl.
6. Add the salad dressing and toss the salad with 2 wooden spoons.

Time
15 minutes

Tools
paper towels
large salad bowl
paring knife
cutting board
2 wooden spoons

Makes
6 servings

Swiss cheese was first made, of course, in Switzerland. Much of the Swiss cheese we eat is made in the United States. Real Switzerland Swiss cheese has a stronger flavor.

Apple Slices with Peanut Butter Dip

Time
15 minutes

Tools
2 small bowls
wooden spoon
cutting board
paring knife
platter

Makes
5 servings

This recipe for peanut butter dip uses a type of tofu called ***silken tofu.*** *Tofu is known as the "cheese of Asia" because it is a cheeselike food made from soybeans, which are very popular in Asia. Silken tofu is a creamy, custardlike product, perfect for dips.*

Ingredients

- ½ cup silken tofu
- ½ cup low-fat cottage cheese
- 3 tablespoons creamy peanut butter
- 1 tablespoon honey
- 1 teaspoon vanilla extract
- 3 large apples
- ½ cup orange juice

Steps

1. In the small bowl, thoroughly mix the tofu, cottage cheese, peanut butter, honey, and vanilla extract.
2. Wash and dry the apples.
3. On the cutting board, use the paring knife to cut the apples in half. Remove the apple cores and seeds. Slice each apple half into ¼-inch slices.
4. Pour the orange juice into the other bowl, and dip each slice into the juice for 1 to 2 seconds. (The juice prevents the apples from turning brown.)
5. Place the bowl of dip in the middle of the platter. Lay the apple slices around the bowl and serve.

CHAPTER 6 SIMPLY RADIANT SKIN, HAIR, AND NAILS

Your skin, hair, and nails make up the **integumentary system.** Skin, the largest organ of the body, covers about 3,000 square inches in the average adult. Little wonder that this system gets so much attention—every day you have to brush your hair, wash your face, take a shower, and so on.

Your skin is between 1 and 6 millimeters thick. A millimeter is the thickness of a dime. Skin is thickest on the part of the body where you need it most, such as the soles of your feet and palms of your hands. It is thinnest in places such as your eyelids and eardrums.

No matter how thick it is, skin consists of two layers: the outer epidermis and the dermis. The **epidermis** is the protective outer layer of skin and is made up mostly of dead cells. The **dermis** is deeper and thicker than the epidermis and is packed with touch-detecting sensors. The living cells in the dermis replace the dead cells in the epidermis.

Besides holding your "insides" in and protecting them from bumps, the skin keeps out harmful substances and helps maintain normal body temperature of 98.6°F (37°C). Your skin also makes a brown-black pigment called **melanin,** which protects you from the sun's ultraviolet rays. By gradually increasing your exposure to the sun, more melanin is produced and your skin tans. Freckles are actually patches of melanin.

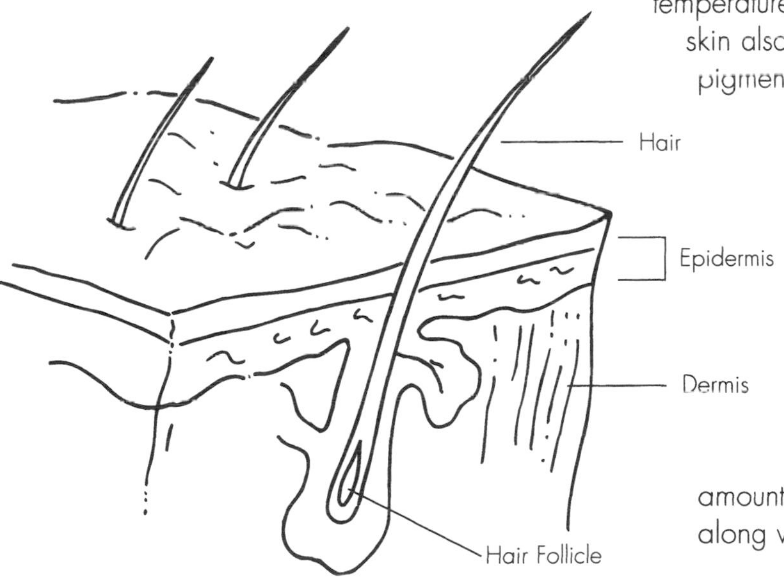

Your skin color is determined by the amount of melanin in your skin, along with two other substances.

Skin colors, such as tan, yellow-tan, cream, or deep brown, are all different shades of brown. There is really no white or black skin. White skin is simply a very light tan, and black skin is a very dark brown.

On your head are about 100,000 hairs. Each hair grows from a **follicle,** or pit, in the skin. Only the hair in the follicle is alive. The visible part of your hair is actually made of dead cells. About 50 hairs fall out each day and are replaced by new hairs. A strand of hair usually lasts for 3 to 4 years before it falls out. Hair grows at the rate of ¼-inch each month, and it grows faster in summer than winter.

Like the skin, hair contains melanin. Varying amounts of melanin produce hair ranging in color from blond to brown to black. The more melanin there is, the darker the hair. A pigment containing iron makes red hair.

Hair has a protective job. Scalp hair and eyebrows protect against sunlight. Your eyelashes and the hair in your nose protect your eyes and nose from airborne particles.

Fingernails and toenails protect, too, because they are quite hard. The hardness of your nails is due to a tough material called **keratin,** which is also found in hair. The white half-moon at the base of your nails is where the nail grows from. Fingernails also help in grasping and picking up small objects.

To see how strong your hair is, try this activity!

HOW STRONG IS MY HAIR?

ACTIVITY

Purpose

To determine whether straight or curly hair is stronger.

Materials

2 strands of hair, one straight and one naturally curly, at least 6 inches long

tape

sandwich-size plastic bag

marbles

STEPS

1. Lay the straight hair out on a flat surface. Tape the plastic bag to one end of the hair.
2. Hold the piece of hair with one hand. Keep your hand still. Start adding marbles, one by one, to the plastic bag. How many marbles can the hair hold before it breaks?
3. Repeat for the curly hair.

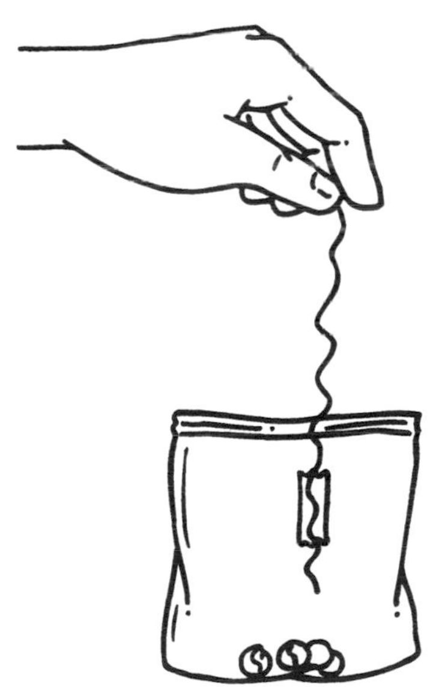

What Happened?

The bag at the end of the straight hair was able to hold more marbles than the curly hair's bag. Straight hair grows out of a round follicle and curly hair grows from a flat follicle. The round shape of the straight hair makes it stronger than the flat, curly hair. Wavy hair—hair that is in between straight and curly—grows from oval follicles.

Vitamins A and C are needed for healthy skin, hair, and nails. The following recipes use ingredients that are high in these vitamins. For example, broccoli, sweet potatoes, carrots, and cantaloupe are great sources of vitamin A. Strawberries, kiwi, cantaloupe, and oranges provide vitamin C.

The Very Best Broccoli-Cheese Strata

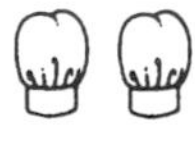

*A **strata** is a casserole usually made by layering bread, cheese, and other ingredients. An egg and milk mixture is then poured over the layers before the strata is baked. Be sure to thaw the frozen broccoli for this recipe ahead of time. You can do this by putting the broccoli in the refrigerator the day before, or by microwaving it.*

Time
30 minutes to prepare
plus
2 hours to refrigerate
plus
50 minutes to bake

Tools
casserole dish
cutting board
paring knife
medium bowl
wooden spoon
waxed paper
plastic wrap
oven mitts
spatula

Makes
6 servings

Ingredients

- vegetable oil cooking spray
- 12 slices whole wheat bread
- 4 eggs
- 2 cups skim or low-fat milk
- 1 tablespoon grated Parmesan cheese
- ¼ teaspoon pepper
- 1 10-ounce package frozen chopped broccoli, thawed, or 2 cups chopped fresh broccoli
- 4 ounces shredded reduced-fat cheddar cheese
- 4 ounces shredded low-fat Swiss cheese

Steps

1. Spray the casserole dish with vegetable oil cooking spray.
2. On the cutting board, cut off the bread crusts with the paring knife. Cut each bread slice in half lengthwise.
3. Break the eggs into the bowl. Add the Parmesan cheese and pepper. Mix well with the wooden spoon.
4. On a 12-inch-long piece of waxed paper, divide the broccoli, cheddar cheese, and Swiss cheese into 4 equal portions. Set aside.

5. Place 6 half-slices of bread on the bottom of the casserole dish. Cover the bread slices with 1 portion of broccoli. Sprinkle with 1 portion of cheddar and Swiss cheese. Repeat the sequence 3 more times, ending with cheese.
6. Pour the egg mixture over the casserole. Cover the dish with plastic wrap and refrigerate overnight or at least 2 hours.
7. Preheat the oven to 350°F.
8. Bake the casserole for 50 minutes or until lightly golden in color. Using oven mitts, remove the casserole from the oven.
9. Cut into 6 servings. Use the spatula to serve.

Brown Sugar Sweet Potato Pie

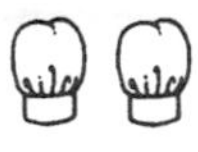

This pie is a favorite in the southern United States. It is not as sweet as pumpkin pie, but looks similar. You can use one 17-ounce can of sweet potatoes instead of boiling fresh sweet potatoes. Simply drain the canned sweet potatoes and mash them.

Time
60 minutes to prepare
plus
25 to 30 minutes to bake

Tools
vegetable peeler
cutting board
paring knife
large pot with lid
colander
oven mitts
large bowl
potato masher
wooden spoon
small bowl
toothpick
wire rack

Makes
1 pie or 8 servings

Ingredients

- 1 pound sweet potatoes (about 3 medium)
- ½ teaspoon salt
- ¼ cup margarine
- 1 teaspoon cinnamon
- ½ teaspoon nutmeg
- ½ teaspoon ground ginger
- ½ cup light brown sugar
- 3 eggs
- 1 cup evaporated skim milk
- 1 9-inch prepared graham cracker pie shell

Steps

1. Preheat the oven to 375°F.
2. Wash and dry the sweet potatoes. Peel them using the vegetable peeler.
3. On the cutting board, use the paring knife to cut each potato into 6 slices.
4. Fill the large pot half full with water. Bring the water to a boil over high heat. Add the salt and potatoes to the boiling water. Cover the pot and cook the potatoes for 40 minutes.
5. Place the colander in the sink. With oven mitts on, drain the sweet potatoes in the colander. Let them cool for 10 minutes.
6. Transfer the potatoes to the large bowl. Mash the potatoes with the potato masher.

7. Cut the margarine into 1-inch pieces and add to the potatoes. Stir the mashed potatoes with a wooden spoon until the margarine has melted.
8. Add the cinnamon, nutmeg, ginger, and brown sugar to the potato mixture. Stir well.
9. Beat the eggs lightly in a small bowl. Finish the pie filling by adding the eggs and milk. Mix well. Pour the mixture into the pie shell.
10. Bake for 25 to 30 minutes or until a toothpick comes out clean when inserted in the center.
11. Cool on a wire rack for 30 minutes. Chill at least 2 hours before serving.

Carrot Rounds with Orange Glaze

This recipe uses fresh carrots that you peel and cut before boiling. If you want to save time, you can boil frozen carrot slices

Time
30 minutes

Tools
vegetable peeler
cutting board
paring knife
large pot
colander
oven mitts
wooden spoon

Makes
6 servings

Ingredients

- 10 medium carrots, or 1¼ pounds frozen sliced carrots
- 3 tablespoons margarine
- 1 tablespoon brown sugar
- ½ teaspoon ground ginger
- 2 tablespoons orange juice

Steps

1. Wash and dry the carrots, then peel them with the vegetable peeler.
2. On the cutting board, use the paring knife to cut the carrots crosswise into ¼-inch thick round pieces.
3. Place the carrots and just enough water to cover them in the large pot.

Ginger is a spice made from the root of a plant. It has a slightly hot flavor.

4. Place the pot over high heat and bring to a boil. Cook the carrots for 10 to 12 minutes until they are tender.
5. Place the colander in the sink. Using oven mitts, bring the pot to the sink and carefully drain the carrots into the colander.
6. Put the carrots back in the pot, and put over medium heat.
7. With the wooden spoon, stir in the margarine, brown sugar, ginger, and orange juice.
8. Once the orange juice mixture boils, it is ready to serve.

Awesome Cantaloupe Sorbet

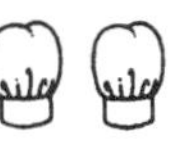

***Sorbet** is a frozen dessert. It is similar to sherbet, except that sorbet is made with water and sherbet is made with milk. Both sorbet and sherbet are often made with fruits. This sorbet recipe uses cantaloupe. To make sorbet (or sherbet), you need an ice cream maker to get the proper texture.*

Ingredients

- 1 medium ripe cantaloupe
- 2 tablespoons sugar
- 1 lemon
- 1 10-ounce package frozen raspberries or 1 pint fresh raspberries
- 1 cup frozen or fresh blueberries
- 1 tablespoon sugar

Steps

1. Wash the outside of the cantaloupe. Then put it on the cutting board and cut it in half. Scoop out all of the seeds with a spoon.

Time
25 minutes to make
plus
1 hour to chill
plus
20 minutes to freeze in ice cream maker

Tools
cutting board
paring knife
spoon
blender or food processor
medium bowl
electric or manual ice cream freezer
colander
paper towels
small bowl
wooden spoon

Makes
4 servings

Because the raspberries and blueberries are a garnish, or decoration, in this recipe, you can substitute other fruit.

2. Scoop out the melon flesh and place into the container of the blender or food processor. Add 2 tablespoons of sugar.
3. Cut the lemon in half, and squeeze the lemon juice over the cantaloupe. Blend the mixture until smooth.
4. Place the cantaloupe puree in the medium bowl and place in your refrigerator for 1 hour to chill.
5. Follow the instructions for your manual or electric ice cream freezer to freeze the cantaloupe mixture.
6. Look at the raspberries and blueberries and remove any that have become moldy. Use a colander to wash and drain the rest of them, and pat them dry with paper towels.
7. Mix the raspberries and blueberries together in the small bowl, then toss with 1 tablespoon of sugar.
8. To serve, place 1 scoop of cantaloupe sorbet in the middle of each plate. Spoon the berries around the sorbet and serve immediately.

Strawberry-Kiwi Cooler

A cooler is a refreshing drink that can cool you down on a warm day. This cooler uses fruit, sherbet, and seltzer to cool and refresh you anytime!

Time
15 minutes

Tools
colander
paper towels
cutting board
paring knife
vegetable peeler
blender

Makes
4 servings

Ingredients

- 4 large strawberries
- 1 kiwi
- 1½ cups raspberry sherbet
- 1 cup raspberry-flavored seltzer
- 4 ice cubes

Steps

1. Put the strawberries in the colander and wash under cold running water. Pat dry with paper towels.
2. On the cutting board, use the paring knife to cut the tops off the strawberries. Cut each berry into 4 pieces.
3. Use the vegetable peeler to carefully peel the fuzzy skin off the kiwi. Slice the kiwi into ¼-inch slices.
4. Place all the fruit in the blender container. Blend thoroughly for 20 seconds.
5. Add the sherbet, seltzer, and ice to the blender and blend well.
6. Pour into 4 glasses and serve.

A kiwi is a fuzzy brown fruit shaped like an egg. When cut open, the inside is green and contains tiny black edible seeds. The sweet taste is something like strawberries, peaches, and melons.

CHAPTER 7 NO-STRESS NERVES

Your nerves carry messages from your brain to your body, sort of like the way telephone wires communicate messages from one place to another. For example, when you want to catch up to a friend, your brain sends a message along your nerves to your leg muscles, telling them to run. Nerves also relay messages in the other direction—from the body to the brain. For instance, if your dog licks your ear, the nerves in your skin send a message to your brain, so you feel the lick.

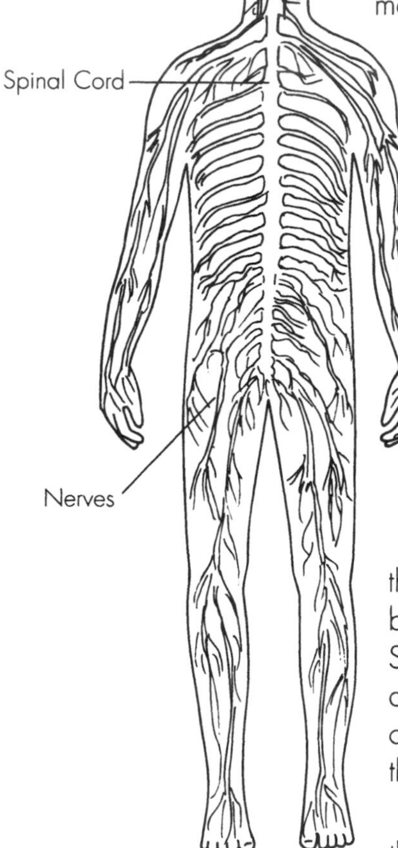

Huge numbers of **nerve cells** are grouped together to make up your **brain.** Protected by the skull bone in your head, the brain is the control center for your body. The brain sends out commands and also receives messages from parts of your body in charge of sensing: the eyes, ears, nose, tongue, and skin. It carries out decisions you make, such as turning the pages in this book, as well as **reflexes** (automatic reactions that happen without your awareness or control), such as breathing. In short, the brain thinks, and it also remembers. The brain's memory is as vast as that of any library.

Attached to your brain is a thick bundle of nerves that goes down the middle of your back to a spot just below your waist. This bundle is called the **spinal cord.** Smaller bundles of nerve cells leave the spinal cord and reach to every part of your body. The brain, spinal cord, and other nerve cells all make up what is called the **nervous system.**

Try the following activity to learn more about how the nervous system operates.

WHY DO MY EYES BLINK?

ACTIVITY

Materials

1 friend or relative

Purpose

To see and understand what a reflex action is.

Steps

1. Ask your friend to stand close to you.
2. Clap your hands loudly about 6 inches from your friend's ear. (Don't get any closer!)

What Happened?

When you clapped your hands, your friend blinked his or her eyes. Blinking in response to a loud noise (or sudden motion) near the eyes is an automatic reaction to protect the eyes from any possible harm. It occurs so fast that you don't even have time to think about it.

Most reflexes protect you from harm, such as when you quickly pull your hand back from something hot. It's amazing reflexes happen so fast when you consider that the loud noise or hot surface is first sensed and relayed to the brain or spinal cord. Then, a message is sent to the muscles to make the reflex action. This is all done in less than a second!

Many members of a group of vitamins, called the ***B vitamins,*** *are necessary for your nervous system to function normally. Each of the following recipes is high in at least one of the B vitamins.*

Brunchtime Ham and Egg Croissant

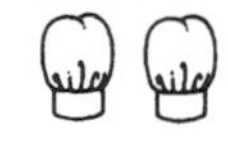

Time
15 minutes

Tools
10-inch nonstick frying pan
cutting board
knife
medium bowl
wire whip
wooden spoon

Makes
4 servings

Canadian bacon is more like ham than bacon in both appearance and flavor.

Brunch is a late-morning meal that includes both breakfast and lunch foods. This recipe is for a lunchtime sandwich filled with scrambled eggs and ham, breakfast foods. Eggs are a good source of vitamin B_{12}.

Ingredients

vegetable oil cooking spray
¼ pound sliced Canadian bacon
6 eggs
⅓ cup skim or low-fat milk
4 croissants

Steps

1. Spray the frying pan with vegetable oil cooking spray.
2. On the cutting board, cut the Canadian bacon into ¼-inch pieces. Set aside.
3. Combine the eggs and milk in the bowl. Beat for 2 minutes with the wire whip.
4. Slice the croissants in half lengthwise.
5. Pour the egg mixture into the frying pan and cook over low to medium heat, without stirring, until the eggs begin to look slightly dry around the edges, about 2 minutes.
6. Lightly stir with a wooden spoon and continue cooking for about 5 minutes. The eggs should look light and fluffy.
7. Add the ham and continue to cook for 3 more minutes. Turn off the heat.
8. Divide the ham and egg mixture into 4 portions. Place one portion on the bottom half of each croissant and cover with the top half to form a sandwich. Serve immediately.

Fabulous Strawberry Crunch

*This recipe is for a type of baked dessert called a **crisp**. A crisp is made of fruit and has a crumbly topping. The flour and oats used to make the topping are good sources of three B vitamins: thiamin, riboflavin, and niacin.*

Ingredients

vegetable oil cooking spray
2 pints strawberries
2 teaspoons lemon juice
3 tablespoons white sugar
1 tablespoon all-purpose flour
1 cup whole wheat flour
½ cup rolled oats
⅓ cup light brown sugar
1 teaspoon cinnamon
4 tablespoons cold margarine

Steps

1. Preheat the oven to 375°F. Spray the baking pan with vegetable oil cooking spray.
2. Put the strawberries in a colander, remove any that are moldy, and rinse the remaining berries well. Pat them dry with paper towels.
3. On the cutting board, slice the tops off the strawberries. Slice each strawberry lengthwise into 4 pieces. Put the berries in the medium bowl.
4. Pour the lemon juice onto the berries. Add the sugar and 1 tablespoon all-purpose flour to the bowl and stir. Place the strawberry mixture in the baking pan.
5. To make the topping, mix the whole wheat flour, oats, brown sugar, and cinnamon in the large bowl.
6. Cut the cold margarine into ¼-inch slices, and put them in the bowl with the flour mixture.

Time
20 minutes to prepare
plus
20 minutes to bake

Tools
9 × 9-inch square baking pan
colander
paper towels
cutting board
knife
medium bowl
wooden spoon
large bowl
pastry blender
or
2 table knives

Instead of strawberries you can substitute 5 cups of sliced and peeled apples, peaches, or pears.

7. Use the pastry blender to blend the ingredients together, rocking it back and forth through the flour mixture. This will take about 3 to 4 minutes. If using 2 table knives, put 1 in each hand and cut one across the other to blend the ingredients together. Make sure the mixture is moist when you are done.
8. Sprinkle the topping over the strawberry mixture.
9. Bake for 20 minutes or until the fruit mixture is bubbly.

Banana and Honey On-the-Go Bread

If you eat your snacks on the go, make this bread on the weekend and you will have something tasty to eat during the week. Any type of bread, such as this one, is a good source of several B vitamins. This bread also contains banana, an excellent source of the mineral ***potassium,*** *which helps nerves send messages.*

Time
25 minutes to prepare
plus
45 minutes to bake

Tools
9 × 5 × 3-inch baking (loaf) pan
small bowl
2 medium bowls
wooden spoon
oven mitts
toothpicks
wire rack

Makes
1 loaf or 16 servings

Ingredients

- vegetable oil cooking spray
- 3 ripe medium bananas
- ½ cup margarine
- ½ cup honey
- 2 eggs
- 2 tablespoons skim or low-fat milk
- 1 cup all-purpose flour
- 1 cup whole wheat flour
- 2 teaspoons baking powder
- ¾ teaspoon salt
- ¼ teaspoon baking soda
- ½ cup chopped walnut pieces

Steps

1. Preheat the oven to 350°F. Spray the loaf pan with vegetable oil cooking spray.
2. Peel the bananas. Break into 1-inch pieces and place in the small bowl.
3. In a medium bowl cream the margarine by pressing it against the sides of the bowl with a wooden spoon until it is light and fluffy.
4. Add the honey to the creamed margarine and continue beating for 50 strokes until the honey dissolves into the margarine.
5. Add the eggs and milk to the margarine mixture and stir until well blended.

6. In the other medium bowl, mix the flours, baking powder, salt, and baking soda until well blended. Set aside.
7. To prepare the batter, add some of the bananas, then some of the flour mixture to the margarine mixture. Beat until smooth.
8. Repeat step 7 until all the banana and all the flour mixture are mixed in well with the margarine mixture.
9. Stir in the walnut pieces.
10. Pour the batter into the prepared pan and bake for 45 minutes.
11. Use oven mitts to pull the pan out of the oven. Insert a toothpick near the center of the bread. If the toothpick comes out clean, the bread is done. If the toothpick has bits of bread on it, the bread is not done and needs to bake 5 more minutes.
12. When the bread is done, place it on a wire rack to cool for 10 minutes.
13. Remove the bread from the pan, using the oven mitts, by turning it upside down over the wire rack. Cool completely before serving.

Baked Buttermilk Spiced Doughnuts

Doughnuts are usually fried in oil. These doughnuts are baked instead. Baked doughnuts contain less fat, but they are very tasty! The milk and flour in this recipe provide several B vitamins.

Time
15 minutes to prepare
plus
20 minutes to bake

Tools
12-cup muffin pan
egg separator
medium bowl
wire whip
oven mitts
wire rack

Makes
12 doughnuts

Ingredients

vegetable oil cooking spray
6 egg whites
1 cup buttermilk
2 teaspoons vegetable oil
½ cup whole wheat flour
½ cup all-purpose flour
⅔ cup powdered sugar
¼ teaspoon ground nutmeg
¼ teaspoon ground cloves
⅛ teaspoon mace
¼ teaspoon cinnamon
¼ cup powdered sugar

Mace is a spice made from the skin that surrounds the nutmeg seed. It is a tannish orange color. Its flavor is stronger and not as sweet as nutmeg.

Steps

1. Preheat the oven to 400°F. Lightly spray the muffin pan with vegetable oil cooking spray.
2. Crack the eggs one at a time into the egg separator over the bowl. Discard the yolks.

3. With the wire whip, whisk the egg whites vigorously until they are frothy, about 1 minute. Add the buttermilk and oil and continue to mix.
4. Add the whole wheat flour, all-purpose flour, powdered sugar, nutmeg, cloves, mace, and cinnamon. Beat the mixture with the wire whip until smooth.
5. Divide the batter evenly between the cups of the muffin pan and bake for 20 minutes. Using oven mitts, remove the pan from the oven. Put the pan on the wire rack and let cool for 1 minute.
6. Using the oven mitts, turn the pan upside down over the wire rack so the doughnuts fall on rack. Let them cool a few minutes, then sprinkle lightly with powdered sugar.

CHAPTER 8 MOVING THROUGH THE DIGESTIVE SYSTEM

Also called the **gastrointestinal tract,** the digestive tract is a hollow tube running down the middle of the body. At the top of the tube is your mouth, where you chew and swallow food. During **digestion,** food is broken down in the digestive tract into **nutrients,** substances in food that are needed to help you grow, to repair your body, and to keep you healthy. Nutrients pass through the walls of the intestines into the blood, a process called **absorption.** Once nutrients are in the blood, they are distributed to the parts of the body where they are needed.

Chewing food is important because it breaks up food into smaller pieces so it can be swallowed. **Saliva** is a watery fluid released into the mouth when you put food into your mouth, or even when you just smell food. Saliva starts the breakdown of certain foods, and helps lubricate the chewed food so it can be swallowed. Food travels from the mouth down a tube called the **esophagus** into the stomach. The **stomach** is a muscular sac that holds about 4 cups of food. Its job is to mix and mash up food.

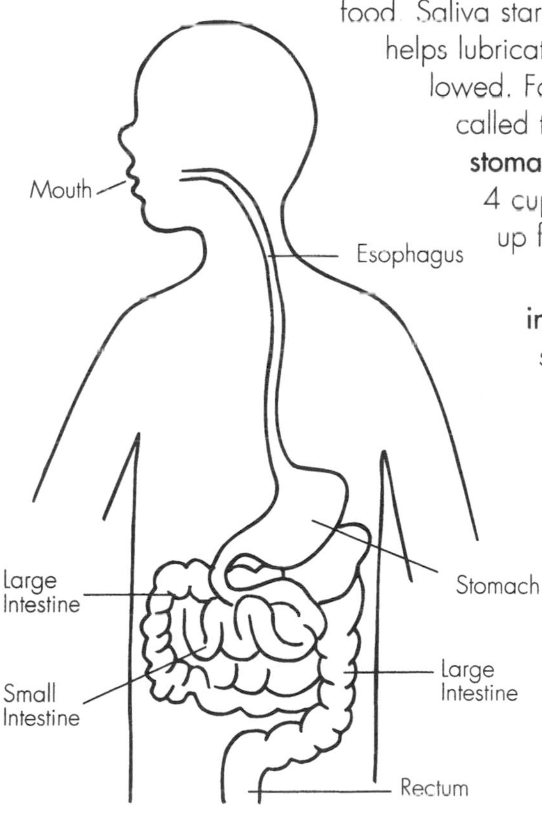

From the stomach, food enters the **small intestine,** then the **large intestine.** The small intestine is about 20 feet long and the large intestine is 4 to 5 feet long. The small intestine got its name because it is smaller in diameter than the large intestine. Much absorption takes place in the intestines. Whatever is not absorbed into the body from the intestines is excreted.

Fiber is a substance in some foods that keeps your digestive system healthy. Do the following activity to learn about why fiber makes you feel full longer.

ACTIVITY

CAN HIGH-FIBER FOODS MAKE ME FEEL FULL?

Purpose

To experience feeling full after eating high-fiber foods.

Materials

high-fiber breakfast cereal containing 5 grams or more of dietary fiber per serving (Look at the "Nutrition Facts" box on the food label for the number of grams of dietary fiber per serving.)

low-fiber breakfast cereal containing 1 gram or less of dietary fiber per serving

notebook

pencil

Steps

1. Read the "Nutrition Facts" on the box of high-fiber cereal to find the serving size. Measure this amount of cereal into a bowl and have it for breakfast in the morning.
2. Write down in your notebook the name of your cereal and what time you ate breakfast.
3. One hour after you eat breakfast, record in your notebook how full you feel by writing a number from 1 to 5. The number "1" means you feel hungry and the number "5" means you feel full.
4. Write down how full you feel again, 2 hours after breakfast, and 3 hours after breakfast.
5. The next morning, eat one serving (check the serving size on the box) of the low-fiber breakfast cereal.
6. Repeat steps 2–4.
7. Compare your fullness ratings for the two mornings.

Nutrition Facts
Serving Size 2 Biscuits (40g)
Servings Per Container 9

Amount per serving	Cereal	with 1/2 Cup Vitamin A & D Fortified Skim Milk
Calories	140	180
Calories from Fat	10	10
	% Daily Value**	
Total Fat 1g*	2%	2%
Saturated Fat 0g	0%	0%
Cholesterol 0mg	0%	0%
Sodium 0mg	0%	3%
Potassium 160mg	5%	10%
Total Carbohydrate 31g	10%	12%
Dietary Fiber 5g	20%	20%
Sugars 0g		
Protein 4g		
Vitamin A	0%	4%
Vitamin C	0%	2%
Calcium	2%	15%
Iron	6%	6%
Vitamin D	0%	10%
Thiamin	6%	8%
Riboflavin	2%	10%
Niacin	10%	10%
Vitamin B6	4%	8%
Folate	4%	6%
Phosphorus	15%	25%
Magnesium	15%	20%
Zinc	8%	8%
Copper	10%	10%

*Amount in Cereal. One half cup skim milk contributes an additional 40 Calories, 65mg Sodium, 6g Total Carbohydrate (6g Sugars) and 4g Protein.

**Percent Daily Values are based on a 2,000 calorie diet. Your daily values may be higher or lower depending on your calorie needs:

		Calories: 2,000	2,500
Total Fat	Less than	65g	80g
Sat Fat	Less than	20g	25g
Cholesterol	Less than	300mg	300mg
Sodium	Less than	2,400mg	2,400mg
Total Carbohydrate		300g	375g
Dietary Fiber		25g	30g

Calories per gram:
Fat 9 • Carbohydrate 4 • Protein 4

Ingredients: 100% Whole Wheat.

Natural Cereal

What Happened?

You probably rated yourself as feeling more full on the morning you ate the high-fiber cereal. Fiber delays how quickly the stomach empties. Therefore you feel full longer. It also means that your body has more time to absorb the other nutrients from the foods you eat. Fiber is abundant in plant foods such as dried beans and peas, fruits, vegetables, whole grains, nuts, and seeds.

Following are some scrumptious high-fiber recipes to keep hunger pangs away!

Rise and Shine Raisin Bran Muffins

Time
20 minutes to prepare
plus
25 minutes to bake

Tools
12-cup muffin pan
2 small bowls
fork
medium bowl
wire whip
liquid measuring cup
wooden spoon
large bowl
ice cream scoop
or
table spoon
oven mitts
wire rack
rubber spatula

Makes
12 muffins

***Bran** is the outer layer of a grain, such as wheat. Bran is high in fiber. This recipe also uses whole wheat flour, which means the flour was made from the whole grain of wheat. Whole wheat flour is a good source of fiber.*

Ingredients

vegetable oil cooking spray
1½ cups bran cereal
½ cup skim or low-fat milk
4 ripe medium bananas
2 eggs
4 tablespoons vegetable oil
½ cup honey
1 cup all-purpose flour
1 cup whole wheat flour
2 teaspoons baking soda
½ teaspoon salt
1 cup raisins

Steps

1. Preheat the oven to 375°F. Lightly spray the muffin pan with vegetable oil cooking spray.
2. In a small bowl, combine the bran cereal and milk. Let stand for 10 minutes until the cereal is soggy.
3. In the other small bowl, break the bananas into small pieces. Using the fork, mash the banana pieces against the sides of the bowl until creamy. Set aside.
4. In the medium bowl, mix the eggs and oil with a wire whip.
5. Spray the liquid measuring cup with vegetable oil cooking spray. Measure ½ cup honey.
6. Add the honey and bananas to the egg mixture. Mix with the wooden spoon until completely blended.
7. In the large bowl, combine the all-purpose flour, whole wheat flour, baking soda, and salt and mix well.

8. Add the egg mixture and bran cereal mixture all at once to the large bowl with the flour mixture.
9. Combine the ingredients just until all the dry ingredients are moistened.
10. Fold in the raisins.
11. Using an ice cream scoop or table spoon, fill each muffin cup two-thirds full with batter.
12. Bake for 25 minutes until golden brown.
13. Use oven mitts to remove the pan from the oven. Place on a wire rack. Let cool for 5 minutes.
14. Loosen the muffins with the rubber spatula. Remove from the pan and place on the wire rack to cool.

Mushroom Barley Soup

Time
20 minutes to prepare
plus
30 minutes to cook

Tools
paper towels
cutting board
paring knife
large pot with lid
wooden spoon
ladle

Makes
6 1-cup servings

Barley is one of the earliest plants known to man. The barley plant produces a grain much like wheat that is full of fiber. It has a mild flavor and is a little chewy. This recipe also uses button mushrooms, another good source of fiber. Button mushrooms are white, cream, or brown in color. Their umbrellas measure from 1 to 3 inches across.

Ingredients

- 8 ounces button mushrooms
- 1 green pepper
- 1 medium onion
- 1 clove garlic
- 2 tablespoons margarine
- ¾ cup quick-cooking barley
- ½ teaspoon ground sage
- ½ teaspoon salt
- 5 cups low-sodium beef broth

Steps

1. Clean the mushrooms by wiping them thoroughly with a dampened paper towel. Cut the mushrooms into ¼-inch slices.
2. Wash the pepper under cold running water. Dry with paper towels.
3. On the cutting board, use the paring knife to cut the green pepper in half. Remove the seeds and cut out the white ribs. Place the pepper halves flat side down and cut into ½-inch lengthwise strips. Cut each strip into ½-inch pieces.
4. Remove the papery outer skin from the onion.
5. On a cutting board, cut the onion in half. Lay each onion half flat on the cutting board and cut into ¼-inch slices.

6. Remove the papery skin from the garlic clove. Slice the garlic. Cut the slices into small pieces.
7. Put the margarine into the large pot and set over medium heat.
8. Cook the mushrooms, green pepper, onion, and garlic in the margarine for about 5 minutes, or until the vegetables are tender but not brown.
9. Stir in the barley, sage, and salt and stir until the barley is coated with the margarine.
10. Add the beef broth to the pot, and bring the soup to a boil.
11. Once the soup is boiling, reduce the heat to low and cover the pot. Simmer the soup for 30 minutes.
12. Ladle the soup into bowls and serve.

Hearty and Healthy Chicken Chili Stew

Time
25 minutes to prepare
plus
30 minutes to cook

Tools
serrated knife
paper towels
cutting board
plastic wrap
paring knife
can opener
large pot
wooden spoon
ladle

Makes
9 1-cup servings

This recipe uses red kidney beans and chickpeas, which are bursting with fiber. Beans and peas are among the highest food sources of fiber.

Ingredients

- 2 pounds skinless, boneless chicken breasts
- 2 green peppers
- 1 medium onion
- 1 garlic clove
- 1 28-ounce can crushed tomatoes
- 1 15-ounce can red kidney beans
- 1 15-ounce can chickpeas
- 2 tablespoons olive oil
- ¾ cup mild salsa
- 1 teaspoon chili powder
- ½ teaspoon ground cumin
- 1 cup shredded reduced-fat cheddar cheese

Steps

1. Wash the chicken in cold water and pat dry with paper towels.
2. Using the serrated knife on the cutting board, cut the chicken lengthwise into ½-inch strips. Cut each strip into 1-inch pieces. Place on a plate and cover with plastic wrap. Put in the refrigerator.
3. Wash the knife and cutting board thoroughly.
4. Wash and dry the green peppers. Remove the papery outer skin from the onion.
5. Cut the onion in half. Lay each onion half flat side down and cut into small pieces.
6. Cut the green peppers in half and remove the seeds and the white ribs with the paring knife. Lay each pepper half flat side down and cut lengthwise into ½-inch strips. Cut each strip into ½-inch pieces.

7. Remove the outer skin from the garlic clove. Cut the garlic clove into slices. Cut the slices into small pieces.
8. Open the can of crushed tomatoes.
9. Open the kidney beans and chickpeas. Drain the liquid from the cans.
10. Put the olive oil in the large pot over low to medium heat.
11. Add the chicken to the pot. Cook and stir constantly with the wooden spoon for 5 minutes.
12. Add the onions, green peppers, and garlic to the chicken. Continue cooking and stirring for 5 more minutes until the chicken loses its pink color and the vegetables are crisp.
13. Add the crushed tomatoes, kidney beans, chick peas, and salsa to the pot and stir well.
14. Add the chili powder and ground cumin to the pot, and stir. Raise the heat to medium and simmer the stew for 20 to 25 minutes
15. Ladle into bowls. Sprinkle with the shredded cheddar cheese.

Fiber-Rich Rice Five Ways

Time
45 minutes

Tools
3-quart saucepan with lid

wooden spoon

Makes
4 servings

Rice is a grain that comes in many forms. This recipe uses brown rice because it has the most fiber. Brown rice gets its color from the bran layers left on the grain. Cooked brown rice has a slightly nutty flavor.

Ingredients

1 cup regular brown rice

Steps

1. Prepare 1 cup of rice according to package instructions.
2. Serve hot or continue with one of these variations.

Variations

Note: After you add the ingredients to the finished rice, stir thoroughly. If the rice has cooled, put the rice over medium heat for 2 minutes to heat thoroughly.

Lemony Rice: Use a grater to shred enough lemon peel (grate the yellow part, not the white part) to make 1 tablespoon. Add the shredded lemon peel and 2 tablespoons lemon juice to the rice.

Spinach and Cheddar Cheese Rice: Add 1 cup of thawed frozen chopped spinach and ½ cup shredded cheddar cheese to the rice.

Tomato-Basil Rice: Wash and dry 1 plum tomato. Cut the tomato into small pieces on a cutting board. Stir the tomato pieces, 1 teaspoon dried basil, and ½ cup shredded mozzarella cheese into the rice.

Southwestern Rice: Add 1 cup salsa, ½ teaspoon chili powder, and ½ cup shredded Monterey Jack cheese.

Rice and Vegetable Medley: Add 10½ ounce package of thawed frozen vegetable assortment.

Autumn Apple Bread Pudding

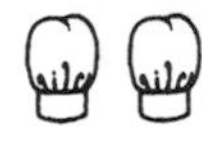

Time
30 minutes to prepare
plus
40 minutes to bake

Tools
vegetable peeler
cutting board
knife
small bowl
small nonstick frying pan
wooden spoon
large bowl
wire whip
2-quart baking dish
oven mitts

Makes
6 servings

When eggs are cooked, the protein in them becomes firm. It is this firmness that gives bread pudding its texture.

Apples, a high fiber food, are used in this recipe for bread pudding. Bread pudding is a baked dessert made from stale bread (to give it a firm texture) and a mixture of eggs, milk, sugar, and spices.

Ingredients

- 1 Granny Smith apple
- 1 teaspoon cinnamon
- 1 teaspoon sugar
- 1 tablespoon margarine
- ½ cup raisins
- 3 eggs
- ½ cup sugar
- 2 cups skim or low-fat milk
- ½ teaspoon cinnamon
- ½ teaspoon ground nutmeg
- ¼ teaspoon ground cloves
- ¼ teaspoon salt
- 2 teaspoons vanilla extract
- 6 slices stale whole wheat bread or ½ loaf stale French bread
- vegetable oil cooking spray

Steps

1. Wash and dry the apple. Peel it with the vegetable peeler. Cut the apple in half on the cutting board, remove the seeds, and core. Slice it into ¼-inch slices.
2. In the small bowl, toss the apple slices with 1 teaspoon cinnamon and 1 teaspoon sugar.
3. Put the margarine in the frying pan over medium heat. When the margarine has melted, add the apples.
4. Cook the apples for 5 minutes until they are tender. Stir with the wooden spoon.
5. Add the raisins to the pan and stir. Take off the heat and set aside to cool.
6. In the large bowl, use a wire whip to whisk the eggs and ½ cup sugar. Whisk until the sugar dissolves.

7. Add the milk, ½ teaspoon cinnamon, nutmeg, cloves, salt, and vanilla to the egg mixture and mix well with the wire whip until frothy.
8. Stir the apple mixture into the egg mixture.
9. On the cutting board with a sharp knife, cut the whole wheat bread into 1-inch cubes. If using French bread, cut into 1-inch slices first.
10. Place the bread cubes in the bowl with the apple and egg mixture, and stir the mixture well. Allow the mixture to stand for 15 minutes.
11. Preheat the oven to 375°F. Spray the baking dish with vegetable oil cooking spray.
12. Pour the bread pudding mixture into the baking dish.
13. Bake pudding for 40 to 50 minutes or until a knife inserted in the center comes out clean.
14. Remove from the oven with oven mitts.

Peanut Butterscotch Popcorn Cutout Squares

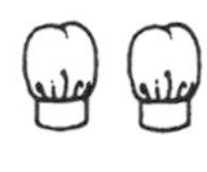

Time
15 minutes
plus
1 hour to set

Tools
large bowl

large frying pan

cookie sheet with 1½-inch sides

serrated knife

Makes
30 squares

Popcorn is a special breed of corn that will expand to 30 to 40 times its original size when you heat it.

If you like peanuts, butterscotch, and popcorn, make this recipe for a great snack. The peanuts and popcorn are good sources of fiber.

Ingredients

10 cups popped popcorn

½ cup margarine

1 10½-ounce bag marshmallows

½ cup peanut butter

½ cup peanuts

10 ounces butterscotch morsels

vegetable oil cooking spray

¼ cup chopped peanuts

Steps

1. Put the popcorn in the large bowl.
2. Put the margarine in the frying pan over medium heat. When the margarine is melted, turn the heat to low and add the marshmallows. Stir constantly until melted.
3. Add peanut butter and stir well. Remove the mixture from the heat and add the warm mixture to the large bowl filled with popcorn.

4. Add the peanuts, stirring until everything is coated.
5. Fold in butterscotch morsels.
6. Spray the cookie sheet with vegetable oil cooking spray.
7. Pour the popcorn mixture onto the cookie sheet, and press it into the pan. If the mixture gets too sticky, dampen your hands with cold water.
8. Sprinkle the chopped peanuts on top.
9. Put the pan in the refrigerator for one hour to set.
10. Cut into squares with the serrated knife and serve.

PART 2 STAYING HEALTHY

As we've seen, the food you eat does many things to keep your body healthy. Follow these three guidelines to stay in super shape!

1. Eat a balanced, varied diet.
2. Eat enough calories, but not too many.
3. Get regular exercise.

These last four chapters will tell you everything you need to know about eating and exercising so you feel healthy and energized for life.

CHAPTER 9
ENTER THE FOOD GUIDE PYRAMID

Welcome to the Food Guide Pyramid! The **Food Guide Pyramid** shows you the kind of foods you need to eat to have a balanced diet. The Pyramid calls for eating a variety of foods to get the nutrients you need to be healthy. If you think of the Pyramid as a real building, it has six rooms (one for each food group, plus one for foods that aren't nutritious). The size of each room shows you what proportion of that food should make up your daily diet.

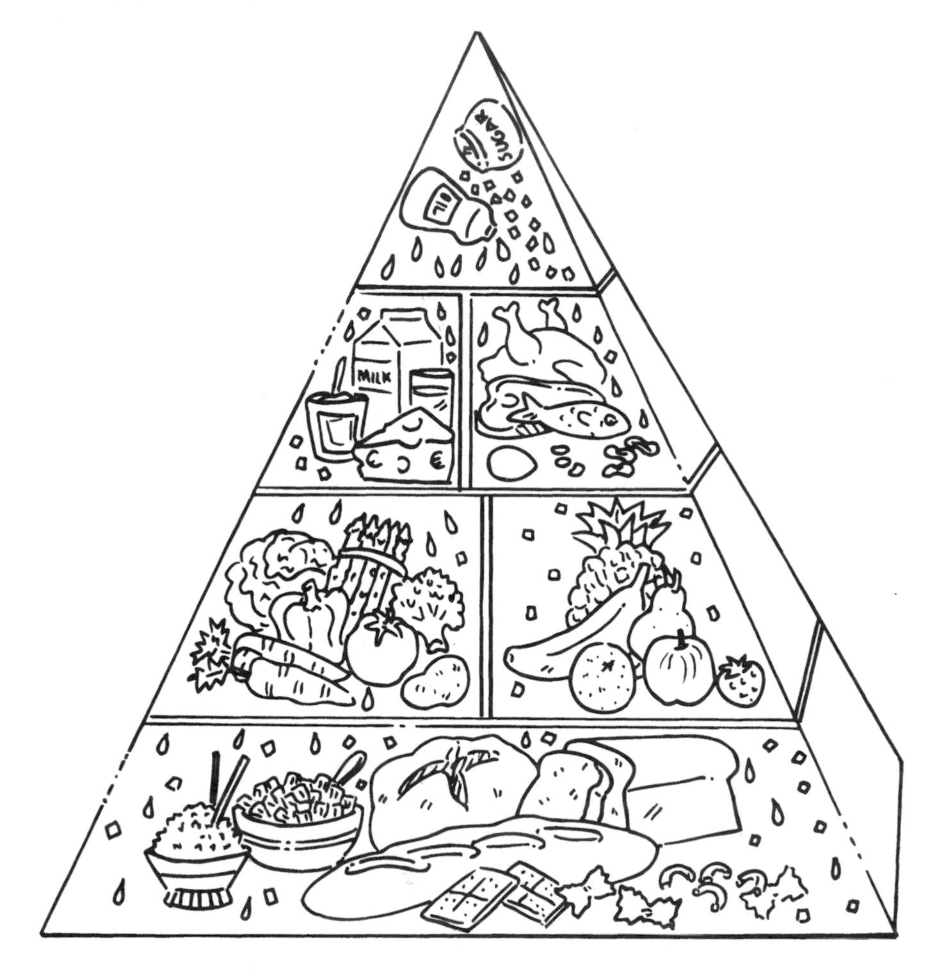

At the base of the Pyramid is a large room for the Bread, Cereal, Rice, and Pasta group. This group gets the biggest room in the Pyramid because you need to eat the largest number of servings each day from these foods: at least six servings. One serving could be 1 slice of bread, 1 bowl of ready-to-eat cereal, or ½ cup of rice or macaroni. The foods in this group supply the nutrient called **carbohydrate.** Carbohydrates are the starches and sugars in food that provide much of the energy the body needs to work and play.

Above the base of the Pyramid are two rooms: one for vegetables and one for fruits. You need to eat at least three servings of vegetables and two servings of fruits each day. One serving of vegetables could be 1 cup of lettuce or ½ cup of cooked vegetables. One serving of fruit could be 1 medium apple or banana or ¾ cup of fruit juice. Vegetables and fruits supply important nutrients called **vitamins** and **minerals,** as well as fiber (as we saw in chapter 8), which do a wide variety of jobs in the body to help us grow and be healthy.

On the third floor of the Pyramid, there are again two smaller rooms: one for the Milk, Yogurt, and Cheese group and one for the Meat, Poultry, Fish, Dry Beans, Eggs, and Nuts group. You need at least three servings from the Milk, Yogurt, and Cheese group each day. A typical serving is 1 cup of milk or yogurt. The milk group provides calcium, which is needed for strong bones and teeth (as discussed in chapter 4).

You need at least two servings from the Meat group daily. One serving could be 2 eggs for breakfast or a hamburger at lunch. The Meat group is rich in protein. Protein, present in all the cells in your body, is needed for the growth and repair of your body (as we saw in chapter 3).

Above the third floor of the Pyramid is an attic. This is where you will find fats, oils, and sweets, such as salad dressings, butter, margarine, sugar, soft drinks, candies, and sweet desserts. These foods do not make up a food group because they supply calories but few nutrients. For this reason, use these foods in small amounts. If you eat too many of these foods, you may not get enough nutrients for proper growth and you may become overweight.

Follow the steps in the activity to see how your diet compares to the Food Guide Pyramid.

DO I EAT THE FOOD PYRAMID WAY? ACTIVITY

Purpose

To compare actual eating with Food Guide Pyramid recommendations.

Materials

notebook

pencil

Steps

1. Make seven columns on your notebook page. Write in the names of the columns as follows: Food Eaten, Bread Group, Vegetable Group, Fruit Group, Milk Group, Meat Group, Fats & Sweets Group.
2. Write down what you ate during one day in the first column (Food Eaten). Start by writing down what you ate in the morning, and continue through the afternoon and evening. Write each food/beverage on a separate line.
3. For the first food on your list, find the correct Food Pyramid column the food belongs in. For example, if the first food on your list is corn flakes, it is a member of the Bread, Cereal, Rice, and Pasta Group. If you are not sure which group the food is in, ask an adult.
4. Compare the serving size of what you ate with the serving sizes in the following list.

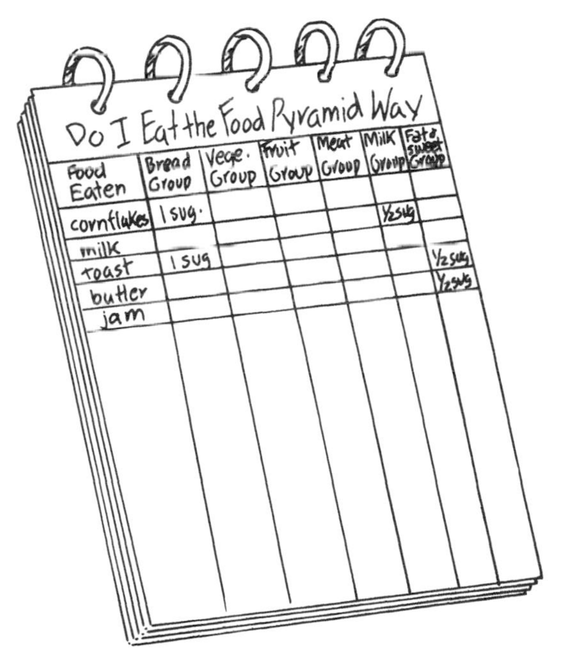

Bread, Cereal, Rice, and Pasta Group

1 slice of bread

1 ounce of ready-to-eat cereal

½ cup of cooked cereal, rice, or pasta

Vegetable Group

1 cup of raw leafy vegetables

½ cup of other vegetables, cooked or chopped raw

⅓ cup of vegetable juice

Fruit Group

1 medium apple, banana, orange

½ cup of chopped, cooked, or canned fruit

¾ cup of fruit juice

Milk Group

1 cup of milk or yogurt

1½ ounces of natural cheese

2 ounces of processed cheese

Meat, Poultry, Fish, Dry Beans, Eggs, and Nuts Group

2 to 3 ounces of cooked lean meat, poultry, or fish

½ cup of cooked dry beans or 1 egg counts as 1 ounce of lean meat

2 tablespoons of peanut butter or ⅓ cup of nuts count as 1 ounce of meat

Estimate how many servings you ate and write it down in the proper column. For example, if you ate about 1 ounce of corn flakes, write down "1 serving" under the Bread Group heading.

5. Do Steps 3 and 4 for each item on your list.
6. Now, add up the total number of servings you ate from each Food Pyramid group. This can be done easily by totaling up all the columns except the first column.

What Happened?

Compare the total number of servings you ate with the Food Guide Pyramid recommendations given on page 107. Did you consume at least the minimum number of servings from each group? If not, think of how you can improve your diet.

The following recipes all use foods from at least two of the Food Pyramid's food groups.

Breakfast No-Bake Granola Bars

Make your own granola bars and pack them to go to school or anywhere!

Time
20 minutes to prepare
plus
30 minutes to cool

Tools
large bowl
wooden spoon
small saucepan
13 × 9-inch baking pan

Makes
18 bars

Ingredients

- 2½ cups toasted rice cereal
- 2 cups quick-cooking oatmeal
- ½ cup raisins
- ½ cup firmly packed brown sugar
- ½ cup light corn syrup
- ½ cup peanut butter
- 1 teaspoon vanilla

Steps

1. Put the rice cereal, oatmeal, and raisins in the bowl and stir together with the wooden spoon.
2. In the small saucepan, mix together the brown sugar and corn syrup. Turn the heat to medium-high. Stir constantly while the mixture is brought to a boil. Once boiling, remove the saucepan from the heat.
3. Stir the peanut butter and vanilla into the sugar mixture in the saucepan. Blend until smooth.
4. Pour the peanut butter mixture over the cereals and raisins in the large bowl. Mix well.
5. Press the mixture into the baking pan.
6. When cool, cut into 18 bars.

Granola is a cereal made of various grains (such as oats), brown sugar or honey, nuts, oil, dried fruits, and sometimes coconut.

Veggie Pockets

Time
20 minutes

Tools
colander

paper towels

vegetable peeler

paring knife

cutting board

Makes
4 sandwiches

This recipe uses pita bread, sometimes called pocket bread. ***Pita bread*** *is a round, flat, Middle Eastern bread that forms a pocket when it is cut in half.*

Ingredients

1 cup cauliflower or broccoli florets

2 carrots

1 green, red, or yellow bell pepper

4 whole wheat pita pockets

½ cup fat-free dressing

Steps

1. Place the cauliflower or broccoli florets in the colander and wash.
2. Wash the carrots and pepper. Pat dry with paper towels.

3. Peel the carrots. Using the paring knife and cutting board, cut off and discard the top and bottom of the carrots. Cut the carrots into ¼-inch slices.
4. Cut the pepper in half. Remove and discard the seeds and ribs. Cut the pepper into ¼-inch long strips.
5. Stuff each pita with some florets, sliced carrots, and pepper strips.
6. Top the vegetables in each pita with 2 tablespoons of the dressing.

Southwestern Macaroni and Cheese

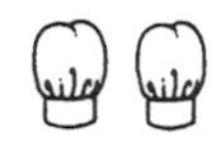

Time
50 minutes

Tools
large saucepan
paring knife
cutting board
colander
small bowl
large, heavy pot
wooden spoon
can opener

Makes
8 servings

The southwestern United States includes Arizona, New Mexico, and Texas. This recipe adds several typically southwestern ingredients to spice up macaroni and cheese. These ingredients, such as beans, tomatoes, and peppers, make this dish very balanced, with a total of four food groups represented.

Ingredients

1½ cups elbow macaroni
1 small green or yellow bell pepper
1 small onion
vegetable oil cooking spray
½ pound extra-lean ground beef
½ pound ground chicken or turkey
1 15-ounce can kidney beans
1 8¾-ounce can whole-kernel corn
1 14½-ounce can chopped tomatoes
1 8-ounce can no-salt-added tomato sauce
1 6-ounce can no-salt-added tomato paste
½ cup water
1 tablespoon chili powder
1 teaspoon ground cumin
¼ teaspoon pepper
1 cup (4 ounces) shredded reduced-fat sharp Cheddar cheese

Steps

1. Fill the large saucepan half full with water. Put on a burner and turn the heat to high.

2. When the water boils, add the macaroni and boil for 10 minutes.

3. While the macaroni cooks, wash the pepper. Use the paring knife and cutting board to cut the pepper in half. Remove and discard the seeds and ribs. Chop the pepper into small pieces.
4. Remove the papery skin from the onion. Cut the onion in half. Lay each onion half flat side down and chop into small pieces.
5. Put the colander in the sink. Slowly pour the boiling macaroni and water through it. Put the macaroni in a small bowl.
6. Spray the large, heavy pot with vegetable oil cooking spray. Put on a burner over medium heat.
7. Add the ground beef and ground chicken or turkey to the pot. Cook about 10 minutes or until the meat browns. Stir during cooking to crumble the meat.
8. Pour the meat into the colander to drain out the fat. Return the meat to the large pot.
9. Add the chopped peppers and onions to the meat. Sauté for 5 minutes over medium heat.
10. Open the cans of kidney beans, corn, tomatoes, tomato sauce, and tomato paste. Drain the liquid from the cans of kidney beans and corn only.
11. Add the contents of the 5 cans to the pot. Also add the cooked macaroni, water, chili powder, cumin, and pepper and stir well.
12. Bring to a boil over a medium-high heat. Once the mixture boils, reduce the heat to low. Simmer for 20 minutes. Stir every few minutes.
13. Spoon onto individual serving plates and top with cheese.

Orange-Sauced Broccoli and Peppers

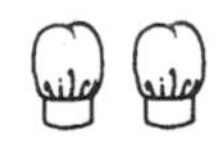

Time
30 minutes

Tools
paring knife
cutting board
medium saucepan
small saucepan
wooden spoon
colander

Makes
4 servings

In this recipe, you use orange juice to make a sauce. Orange sauce makes vegetables taste excellent, and you get to add a fruit group to your veggie group!

Ingredients

- 1 medium red or yellow bell pepper
- 1 cup water
- 1 pound fresh or frozen broccoli spears
- 1 small onion
- ½ tablespoon margarine
- 1½ teaspoon cornstarch
- ⅔ cup orange juice
- 2 teaspoons Dijon-style mustard

Steps

1. Using the paring knife on the cutting board, cut the pepper in half. Remove and discard the seeds and ribs. Cut the pepper into 1-inch squares.
2. In the medium saucepan, heat 1 cup of water to boiling. Once boiling, add the broccoli and pepper. Cook for 8 to 10 minutes, or until the broccoli is tender when pierced with a fork.
3. While the vegetables are cooking, make the sauce. Take the papery outside off the onion. Using the paring knife and cutting board, cut it in half. Lay each onion half flat side down and chop into small pieces.
4. Put the margarine in the small saucepan over medium heat. When the margarine is melted, add the onion and cook until it is tender.
5. Stir in the cornstarch. Add the orange juice and mustard. Cook and stir constantly until the mixture is thickened and bubbly. Cook and stir 2 minutes more. The sauce is now ready.

6. When the vegetables are done, put a colander in the sink and slowly pour the boiling water and vegetables into the colander. Once the water is completely drained, put the vegetables back into the saucepan.
7. Spoon the sauce over the broccoli and peppers. Serve.

Gingersnappy Peach Crisp

Time
15 minutes
plus
20 minutes to bake

Tools
8-inch square baking pan
resealable plastic bag
medium bowl
2 table knives
can opener
oven mitts

Makes
6 servings

Gingersnaps are flavored with ginger and molasses. Molasses is a thick, brown syrup made from sugar cane. Gingersnap cookies are low in fat compared to many other varieties.

Peach crisp is like peach pie, only there is no crust. Instead a crumb topping is used. This topping includes crushed gingersnap cookies to give the dish an original flavor.

Ingredients

vegetable oil cooking spray
8 gingersnap cookies
2 tablespoons brown sugar
½ teaspoon ground cinnamon
1 tablespoon margarine
2 16-ounce cans peach slices in fruit juice, drained, or 5 fresh peaches
frozen yogurt (optional)

Steps

1. Preheat the oven to 375°F.
2. Spray the baking pan with vegetable oil cooking spray.

3. Put the cookies into the plastic bag and close tightly. Crush them with your hands.
4. Put the crushed gingersnaps, brown sugar, and cinnamon in the bowl. Add the margarine.
5. Hold a table knife in each hand and draw the knives across each other to cut the margarine into the dry ingredients. Keep cutting until the mixture is crumbly.
6. Open the 2 cans of peaches. Drain the liquid. If using fresh peaches, wash them. Use a paring knife to remove the skin, and cut into ¾-inch slices.
7. Arrange the peaches in the baking dish. Then sprinkle the gingersnap mixture over the peaches.
8. Bake for 20 minutes or until thoroughly heated. Remove from the oven using oven mitts. Serve warm or at room temperature, with frozen yogurt if desired.

CHAPTER 10

NO MORE COUCH POTATO!

Which of the following statements about exercise are true?

- Exercising makes you tired.
- You have to be athletic to exercise.
- Exercising must be intense and exhausting to have any benefits.
- Exercising is not fun.
- Exercising takes too much time.

The answer is, none of them. Instead of causing tiredness, regular, brisk exercise gives most people more energy than before. Many activities, such as walking or biking, do not require any special athletic abilities. They also do not have to be done to the point where you are exhausted. It's important to find an activity (or two) that you enjoy—in-line skating, gymnastics, dancing—so that you'll do it more often.

By making fitness a part of everyday life, you will always have time for it! Try walking the dog, washing the car, biking to school or to a friend's house, playing basketball in the driveway, running to the store for milk, or swimming in the neighborhood pool. Although team sports are often great ways to get exercise, sports such as dance or horseback riding are also wonderful to get the body moving!

There are benefits experienced by people of all ages who exercise regularly. Regular exercise builds and tones muscles. It also helps you maintain a healthy body weight. Your heart works better and you feel better about yourself.

Many foods can help give you more energy for exercise. One kind of food designed specifically for people who exercise is the "sports drink." To learn more about what sports drinks are made of, try the following activity.

WHAT'S IN A SPORTS DRINK?

ACTIVITY

Purpose

To make your own sports drink and compare it to a commercial brand of sports drinks.

Materials

1 small can frozen lemonade

pitcher

wooden spoon

2 glasses

1 bottle commercial sports drink, such at Gatorade™

Steps

1. Make the lemonade according to the package instructions.
2. Pour ½ cup of lemonade into a glass. Add ½ cup of water to make dilute lemonade.
3. Read the ingredients label on the bottle of sports drink.
4. Pour a glass of the bottled sports drink.
5. Drink some of the dilute lemonade and some of the sports drink.

What Happened?

Sports drinks are beverages that contain small amounts of sugar, sodium and potassium (two minerals that you lose when you sweat), and sometimes additional ingredients. Most are designed to be used during long exercise periods of 90 minutes or more. Sports drinks help replace water and minerals lost during long exercise periods. They also provide a small amount of sugar, which can be burned for energy. If you look on the Gatorade food label, you will find the words "sodium," "potassium," and "glucose." Glucose is a form of sugar.

Long before sports drinks were available at the supermarket, athletes had their own homemade sports drinks: flat or defizzed cola, tea with honey, and dilute lemonade. These drinks also provide water, sugar, and some minerals. In this activity, you made your own sports drink: dilute lemonade. Which did you prefer to drink: the lemonade or the bottled sports drink?

Carbohydrates are the most important fuel source for exercise. Carbohydrates are a group of nutrients that includes sugar, starch, and fiber. Try one of the following high-carbohydrate recipes to give you plenty of energy for exercise.

Awesome Banana Berry Pancakes

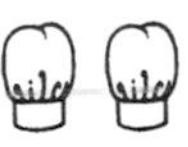

Bananas and berries makes great pancakes! Bananas are also loaded with potassium. This recipe calls for raspberries but you can substitute any other type of berry, fresh or frozen.

Time
20 minutes

Tools
large bowl

2 small bowls

fork

wooden spoon

colander

griddle
or
frying pan

ladle

spatula

Makes
12 4-inch pancakes

Ingredients

- 1 cup all-purpose flour
- 1 cup whole wheat flour
- 1 tablespoon baking powder
- ½ teaspoon cinnamon
- ¼ teaspoon ground nutmeg
- ¼ cup sugar
- 1 large ripe banana
- 2 large eggs
- 1¼ cups skim or low-fat milk
- ⅓ cup vegetable oil
- ½ teaspoon vanilla extract
- 1 cup raspberries
- vegetable oil cooking spray
- pancake syrup or jelly

Steps

1. Mix the all-purpose flour, whole wheat flour, baking powder, cinnamon, nutmeg, and sugar in the large bowl.
2. Mash the banana in a small bowl, using the tines of a fork to press it against the sides of the bowl until creamy. Set aside.
3. Crack the eggs into the other small bowl. Beat lightly with the fork.
4. Add the banana, eggs, milk, oil, and vanilla extract to the flour mixture. Stir with the wooden spoon until just blended.
5. Discard any raspberries that have become moldy. Then wash the rest of the berries in the colander and drain well. Fold them gently into the batter.
6. Spray the griddle or frying pan with vegetable oil cooking spray, and place it over medium heat for 1 minute.

7. Using the ladle, pour enough batter on the griddle or frying pan to make a 4-inch pancake.
8. When bubbles appear and the pancake is golden brown underneath, turn with the spatula and cook the other side of the pancake for about 1 minute, until it is golden brown and cooked underneath. Stack pancakes on plate to keep warm.
9. Serve immediately with syrup or jelly.

Tricolor Spiral Pasta with Fresh Garden Veggies

Pasta is an excellent source of carbohydrates, as well as some vitamins and minerals. This great salad can be made ahead of time and refrigerated. Just remember to add the salad dressing just before serving.

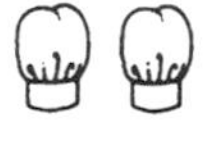

Time
30 minutes

Tools
paper towels
cutting board
knife
vegetable peeler
large salad bowl
wooden spoon
large pot
colander
oven mitts
small bowl
wire whip
serving spoons

Makes
6 servings

Ingredients

- 1 green pepper
- 2 plum tomatoes
- 1 cucumber
- 1 yellow squash
- 2 scallions
- 1 pound tri-color rotini or spiral shaped pasta
- 8 ounces reduced-fat mozzarella cheese
- ¼ cup olive oil
- 3 tablespoons lemon juice
- 2 teaspoons dried basil
- ½ teaspoon black pepper

Steps

1. Wash and dry the pepper, tomatoes, cucumber, squash, and scallions.
2. Using the knife and cutting board, cut the pepper in half. Remove and discard the seeds and the white ribs. Lay the pepper halves cut side down on the cutting board. Cut lengthwise into ½-inch strips. Cut each strip into bite-sized pieces.
3. Slice the tomatoes into ¼-inch slices.
4. Peel the cucumber with the vegetable peeler. Cut the cucumber into thin slices and then cut each slice in half.
5. Cut the yellow squash into thin slices. Cut each slice in half.
6. Cut off and discard the roots and wilted leaf ends of the scallions. Cut into ¼-inch slices.
7. Place all of the vegetables into the large salad bowl. Mix with the wooden spoon.

8. Fill the large pot two-thirds full with water. Place on a burner on high and bring the water to a boil. Add the pasta and cook according to the directions on the package.
9. Place the colander in the sink. When the pasta is finished cooking, use oven mitts to pour the pasta slowly into the colander.
10. Run cold water over the pasta to cool it down. Put the cooled, drained pasta into the salad bowl and toss with the fresh vegetables.
11. On the cutting board, cut the mozzarella cheese into ½-inch cubes. Add the cheese to the pasta and vegetables.
12. Put the olive oil, lemon juice, dried basil, and black pepper in the small bowl and whisk with the wire whip to mix well. Add dressing to the pasta salad and toss well with serving spoons.

Pick-Me-Up Power-Packed Lasagna

This is probably the only lasagna recipe that doesn't use lasagna noodles. Instead, it uses corn tortillas, and they are great!

Time
25 minutes to prepare
plus
30 minutes to bake

Tools
13 × 9 × 2-inch baking pan
large frying pan
wooden spoon
large bowl
can opener
medium bowl
fork
spoon
oven mitts
wire rack

Makes
12 servings

Ingredients

- vegetable oil cooking spray
- 1 pound lean ground turkey
- 1 17-ounce can low-sodium whole-kernel corn
- 1 15-ounce can tomato sauce
- 1 cup mild salsa
- 1½ tablespoons chili powder
- 1 teaspoon ground cumin
- 2 eggs
- 1 16-ounce container low-fat ricotta cheese
- ¼ cup grated Parmesan cheese
- 1 teaspoon dried oregano
- 12 flour tortillas
- 1 cup reduced-fat shredded Cheddar cheese

Steps

1. Preheat the oven to 375°F. Spray the baking pan with vegetable oil cooking spray and set it aside.
2. Spray the large frying pan with vegetable oil cooking spray.
3. Put the ground turkey in the frying pan over medium heat. Cook the turkey, breaking it up with the wooden spoon, for about 5 to 8 minutes, until all of the light pink color has disappeared. Take the pan off the heat. Drain the meat and set aside in the large bowl.
4. Open the can of corn and drain off the liquid. Open the tomato sauce.
5. Add the corn, tomato sauce, salsa, chili powder, and ground cumin to the cooked turkey. Mix well with the wooden spoon.
6. Crack the eggs into the medium bowl and mix lightly with the fork.

Chili powder is a blend of mild chili peppers, oregano, garlic, salt, and cumin. Cumin is a spice with a slightly bitter flavor.

7. Add the ricotta cheese, Parmesan cheese, and oregano to the eggs. Mix thoroughly.
8. To make the lasagna, arrange 6 tortillas on the bottom and up the sides of the baking pan.
9. Using a spoon, top the tortillas with half of the meat mixture.
10. Spoon all of the ricotta cheese mixture over the meat and spread it evenly.
11. Arrange the remaining tortillas over the top of the cheese.
12. Top the tortillas with the remaining meat mixture.
13. Sprinkle the cheddar cheese evenly over the top of the lasagna.
14. Bake for 30 minutes until hot and bubbly.
15. Using oven mitts, remove the pan from the oven and place on a wire rack. Let stand 10 minutes before cutting.

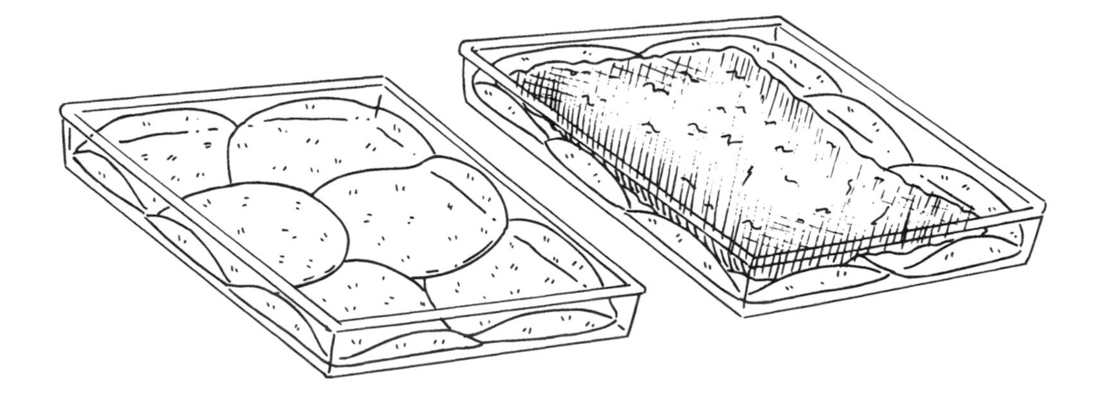

Energizing Apple-Oatmeal Squares with Raisins

This is an easy recipe for a quick energy snack you can carry anywhere.

Time
20 minutes to prepare
plus
30 minutes to bake

Tools
8-inch square baking pan
vegetable peeler
paring knife
cutting board
small bowl
fork
large bowl
wire whip
wooden spoon
oven mitts
wire rack
serrated knife

Makes
12 servings

Squares Ingredients

vegetable oil cooking spray
1 apple
3 eggs
1 teaspoon salt
1 cup sugar
½ cup vegetable oil
½ cup raisins
1 teaspoon cinnamon
½ teaspoon ground nutmeg
¼ teaspoon ground cloves
3 cups rolled oats (not quick-cooking)
1 cup skim or low-fat milk

Topping Ingredients

½ teaspoon ground nutmeg
1 teaspoon sugar

Steps

1. Preheat the oven to 350°F.
2. Spray the baking pan with vegetable oil cooking spray.
3. Using the vegetable peeler, peel the apple.
4. Using the paring knife and cutting board, cut the apple in half. Remove the seeds and core. Place the halves flat side down and cut the apple into bite-size pieces.
5. Crack the eggs into the small bowl. Mix lightly with the fork.
6. In the large bowl, whisk the eggs, salt, sugar, and oil together with the wire whip. Whisk for about 1 minute until the mixture is thick and creamy.

7. Add the apple pieces, raisins, cinnamon, nutmeg, and cloves to the egg mixture.
8. Add the oatmeal and milk to the egg mixture. Mix well with the wooden spoon. Allow the mixture to sit in the bowl for 15 minutes at room temperature so the oatmeal can absorb the liquid in the bowl.
9. Pour the mixture into the baking pan. Make the topping: mix ½ teaspoon of nutmeg with 1 teaspoon of sugar. Sprinkle the nutmeg sugar on top of the oatmeal mixture.
10. Bake for 30 to 35 minutes until the top is lightly golden brown. Remove the pan from the oven with oven mitts.
11. Cool on a wire rack for 20 minutes. Cut into squares with a serrated knife. Serve warm.

Blueberry Power-Snack Turnovers

If you like to get your hands into dough, this recipe gives you lots of opportunities! Try your hand at making a dozen custom-made turnovers.

Ingredients

vegetable oil cooking spray
1½ cups all-purpose flour
1 cup whole wheat flour
1 tablespoon baking powder
¼ teaspoon ground nutmeg
¼ teaspoon cinnamon
½ teaspoon salt
4 tablespoons margarine
1 cup skim or low-fat milk
additional flour for kneading and rolling out dough
½ cup all-fruit spreadable blueberry jam
1 egg
1 tablespoon water
¼ cup wheat germ

Steps

1. Preheat the oven to 350°F.
2. Spray the cookie sheet with vegetable oil cooking spray.
3. In the medium bowl, mix together the all-purpose flour, whole wheat flour, baking powder, nutmeg, cinnamon, and salt. Set aside.
4. Put the margarine in the saucepan over medium heat. Slowly melt the margarine, stirring it constantly with the wooden spoon.
5. Add the melted margarine and the milk to the flour mixture. Stir together until the mixture forms a dough.
6. **Knead** the dough on a lightly floured surface (such as a pastry board or cutting board) for 4 minutes. Knead by pressing the dough out. Then fold in half and give the dough a quarter turn. Repeat.

Time
30 minutes to prepare
plus
20 minutes to bake

Tools
cookie sheet
medium bowl
3-quart saucepan
wooden spoon
pastry board
or
cutting board
rolling pin
paring knife
sandwich spreader
or
table knife
egg separator
small bowl
2 table forks
pastry brush
oven mitts

Makes
12 turnovers

You can substitute any other type of jam for blueberry in this recipe.

7. Lightly flour the rolling pin and flat surface. With the rolling pin, gently roll out the dough until it is about ½-inch thick, approximately 12 inches by 16 inches.
8. Using the paring knife, cut out 12 4-inch square pieces of dough.

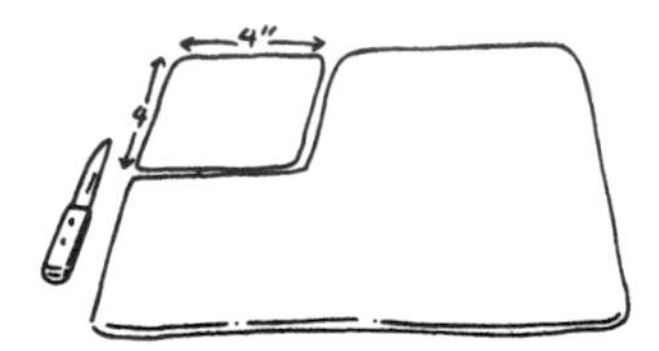

9. Using a sandwich spreader or table knife, spread 1 tablespoon of blueberry jam onto each dough square, leaving a ¼-inch border around the edges of each square.
10. Crack the egg into the egg separator placed over the small bowl. The egg white will go into the bowl. Discard the yolk.
11. Use a table fork to mix the egg white with 1 table-spoon of water.

12. Using the pastry brush, lightly brush the borders of the squares with the egg white mixture. Fold the square in half lengthwise to form a triangle. Press down well to seal. Reinforce the seal by pressing along all sides with the tines of the fork.
13. Lightly brush the tops of the turnovers with the egg white mixture. Place turnovers 2 inches apart on the cookie sheet. Sprinkle the tops with wheat germ.

14. Bake for 20 minutes until turnovers are golden brown. Remove from the oven with oven mitts. Allow the turnovers to cool for 10 minutes before eating.

CHAPTER 11 MAINTAINING A HEALTHY WEIGHT

Did an adult ever ask you where you get all your energy from? The next time someone asks you that question, be sure to explain that your energy comes from eating. Foods contain energy, called **calories,** that your body uses to run, breathe, grow, stay healthy, and stay alive. Different foods contain varying amounts of calories.

When you eat more calories than your body needs, you gain weight. Being overweight is not healthy for children or adults. If you are overweight, you can lose weight by doing two things: eating fewer calories and exercising more. Physical activity is an important way to use food energy. To burn calories, spend less time watching television or playing computer games. Instead, find an activity or sport you like. It can be as simple as biking or skating. Exercise not only helps you lose weight but also helps avoid gaining it back. Chapter 10 gives more information on exercising.

Check out the following tips to eat fewer calories.

- Making lower-calorie snack choices is a great place to start. Instead of a candy bar, enjoy a chocolate granola bar. Eat pretzels, popcorn, or baked potato chips instead of regular potato chips. Low-fat frozen yogurt and frozen juice bars have fewer calories than regular ice cream. Healthier cookie choices include graham crackers, animal crackers, and gingersnaps.
- For sandwich toppings, try lettuce, tomato, onion, pickles, mustard, and ketchup instead of high-calorie toppings like cheese, bacon, margarine, or mayonnaise (unless low-fat).
- Eat cheese pizza plain or with vegetable toppings like peppers or onions. Sausage, pepperoni, and extra cheese pizzas contain a lot more calories.
- Make sure you eat at least three servings of vegetables and two servings of fruits each day.
- Drink 1% or skim milk. They both contain fewer calories than regular or 2% milk.
- Instead of drinking regular soft drinks, try fruit-flavored seltzer water, or diet soft drinks. Mixing seltzer with fruit juice makes a great drink, too.

The following activity will help you learn how many calories are in some of your favorite foods.

WHICH FOOD HAS FEWER CALORIES?

Materials

notebook

pencil

Purpose

To identify alternatives to high-calorie foods.

Steps

1. Write down each of these pairs of food in your notebook.

a.	Double-decker burger with special sauce	Cheeseburger
b.	Baked potato	Medium French fries
c.	Slice of cheese pizza	Slice of pepperoni pizza
d.	Onion rings	Mixed vegetables
e.	2 chocolate chip cookies	1 apple
f.	Turkey sandwich with lettuce and tomato	Turkey sandwich with cheese and mayonnaise
g.	½ cup ice cream	½ cup fruit ice
h.	12-ounce can of cola	1 cup apple juice
i.	1 ounce potato chips	1 ounce pretzels
j.	½ bagel with margarine	½ bagel with jelly

2. Circle the food in each pair that you think has fewer calories.

What Happened?

Check your answers with these.

a. Cheeseburger. If you go to McDonald's, their double-decker burger (Big Mac) has 560 calories, but their cheeseburger has only 310 calories.

b. Baked potato. A baked potato is about 250 calories while a medium order of French fries is 320 calories.

c. Cheese pizza. A slice of cheese pizza has about 250 calories, while a slice of pepperoni pizza has about 275 calories.

d. Mixed vegetables. A ½ cup serving of mixed vegetables has only 50 calories. Seven onion rings have 285 calories!

e. Apple. Two chocolate chip cookies have about 120 calories, while a medium apple has only 70 calories.

f. Turkey sandwich with lettuce and tomato. Lettuce and tomato add almost no calories to the sandwich, but a slice of cheese and a tablespoon of mayonnaise add more than 100 calories.

g. Fruit ice. A half cup of fruit ice is less than 100 calories. A half cup of vanilla ice cream varies from 130 calories to more than 200 calories.

h. Apple juice. A 12-ounce can of cola has about 150 calories. One cup of apple juice has about 110 calories.

i. Pretzels. One ounce of potato chips has about 150 calories compared to 110 calories for pretzels.

j. Bagel with jelly. Margarine has 100 calories per tablespoon, whereas jelly has only 50.

The following recipes are all designed to be low in calories. Try them out and see for yourself how delicious healthy food can be.

Trimline Blueberry and Nutmeg Muffins

Homemade muffins are nutritious and can satisfy a desire for sweets without all the calories of a frosted cake.

Time
15 minutes to prepare
plus
20 minutes to bake

Tools
12-cup muffin pan
colander
large bowl
medium bowl
wooden spoon
ladle
oven mitts
wire rack
rubber spatula

Makes
12 muffins

Ingredients

vegetable oil cooking spray
1 cup fresh or frozen blueberries
1 cup all-purpose flour
1 cup whole wheat flour
¼ cup sugar
1 tablespoon baking powder
¼ teaspoon salt
½ teaspoon cinnamon
¼ teaspoon ground nutmeg
1 egg
1 cup skim or low-fat milk
¼ cup vegetable oil

Steps

1. Preheat the oven to 400°F.
2. Spray the muffin cups with vegetable oil cooking spray.
3. Put the blueberries in a colander. Wash and drain well. Set aside.
4. Mix the all-purpose flour, whole wheat flour, sugar, baking powder, salt, cinnamon, and nutmeg in the large bowl.

Muffins are an example of a group of baked goods called quick breads. While white bread and whole-wheat bread need yeast to make them rise, which takes a lot of time, quick breads use baking power. Baking powder makes muffins rise quickly in the oven.

5. Mix the egg, milk, and vegetable oil in the medium bowl.
6. Add the milk mixture all at once to the flour mixture in the large bowl.
7. With the wooden spoon, combine the ingredients just until all dry ingredients are moistened. Fold in the blueberries.
8. Using the ladle, fill each muffin cup two-thirds full with batter.
9. Bake for 20 minutes or until golden brown.
10. Using oven mitts, remove pan from oven. Place on a wire rack. Let cool for 5 minutes.
11. Loosen the muffins with the rubber spatula and remove from pan.

Spicy Chicken and Cheese in Pita Pouch

White meat chicken, without the skin, is naturally low in calories. This recipe combines chicken, salsa, and reduced-fat cheese to make a delicious lunch or light supper.

Time
20 minutes

Tools
paper towels
paring knife
cutting board
10-inch nonstick frying pan
wooden spoon

Makes
4 sandwiches

Ingredients

- 1 whole skinless, boneless chicken breast
- 1 tablespoon olive oil
- ½ cup mild thick-and-chunky salsa
- 2 whole wheat pita breads
- ½ cup reduced-fat grated Monterey Jack cheese

Steps

1. Wash chicken in cold water and pat dry with paper towels.
2. Using the paring knife and cutting board, cut the chicken lengthwise into ½-inch strips. Cut each strip into ½-inch cubes. Wash the knife and the board thoroughly.
3. Put the olive oil in the frying pan over medium heat.
4. Add the chicken and cook for about 5 minutes, stirring with a wooden spoon, until the chicken is lightly browned.
5. Stir the salsa into the chicken. Cook until the salsa is heated through. Turn off the heat.
6. Cut the pita breads in half. Spoon the chicken mixture evenly into the pita pockets. Top the filling with Monterey Jack cheese. Serve immediately.

Fruit Combo Roll-Ups

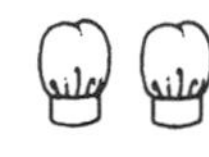

Time
30 minutes to prepare
plus
3 hours to cook

Tools
cookie sheet
cutting board
knife
2 small dishes
blender
medium bowl
1-cup liquid measuring cup
sandwich spreader
or
table knife
oven mitts
spatula
resealable plastic bags

Makes
10 rolls

•••••

Mace is a spice that comes from the nutmeg tree. It tastes stronger than nutmeg, and is not as sweet.

•••••

Try this recipe to make your own fruit leather without adding any sugar. It takes some time to cook it at low temperature in the oven, but it's worth the wait!

Ingredients

vegetable oil cooking spray
1 lemon
½ teaspoon mace
5 ounces frozen peaches, thawed, or 2 fresh peaches
5 ounces frozen strawberries, thawed, or 1 cup fresh strawberries

Steps

1. Preheat the oven to 175°F.
2. Spray the cookie sheet with vegetable oil cooking spray.
3. Using the cutting board, cut the lemon in half.
4. Divide the mace equally between the 2 small dishes.
5. If using fresh fruit, wash and pat dry the peaches and strawberries. On the cutting board, use a paring knife to remove the skin from the peaches. Cut the peaches into ¾-inch slices. Next, cut the tops off the strawberries. Slice each strawberry lengthwise.
6. Put the peaches in the blender container. Squeeze the juice from a lemon half into the blender. Add a portion of mace. Blend the mixture on high until smooth, about 1 minute. Pour the mixture into the medium bowl.
7. Wash and thoroughly dry the blender container. Put the strawberries into the blender container. Squeeze the juice of the other half of the lemon into the blender and add the remaining mace. Blend the mixture on high until it is smooth, about 1 minute.

8. Using a sandwich spreader or table knife, spread 1 cup of the peach mixture thinly over half of the cookie sheet.
9. Spread 1 cup of the strawberry mixture thinly over the remaining part of the cookie sheet. Overlap the 2 mixtures by 1 inch.
10. Bake with the oven door slightly open for about 3 hours. After two hours, use oven mitts to remove the cookie sheet from the oven. Check to see if the fruit leather is dry enough to peel off the cookie sheet. If it is, proceed to step 11. If it is still slightly wet, put it back in oven for another hour. If still wet at the 3-hour mark, use a spatula to flip it over. Then return to the oven for 10 more minutes.
11. Take the cookie sheet out of the oven using oven mitts. Peel the fruit roll from the cookie sheet and place it on a clean cutting board.
12. Cut the combo roll crosswise into strips with a knife. Roll up the strips. When cool, store in resealable plastic bags.

Rice-Cake Mini-Sandwich Snacks

Time
1 hour to warm cream cheese
plus
15 minutes

Tools
cutting board
paring knife
medium bowl
colander
paper towel
hand-held electric mixer
sandwich spreader
or
table knife

Makes
4 servings

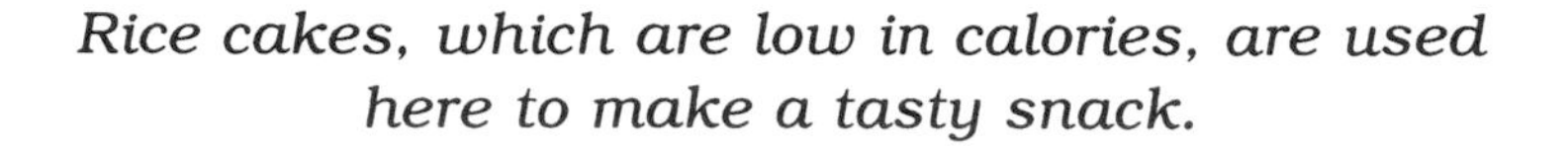

Rice cakes, which are low in calories, are used here to make a tasty snack.

Ingredients

- 4 ounces light or fat-free cream cheese
- 4 strawberries
- ¼ cup strawberry preserves
- 1 tablespoon confectioner's sugar
- 8 mini-rice cakes

Steps

1. Using the cutting board and paring knife, cut the cream cheese into 1-inch cubes. Place the cubes in the bowl and set aside at room temperature for 1 hour.
2. Place the strawberries in a colander and wash. Pat dry with a paper towel.
3. On the cutting board, cut the tops off the strawberries. Cut the strawberries in half.
4. With the electric mixer on low speed, beat the softened cream cheese for one minute until it is light and fluffy.
5. Add the strawberry preserves and confectioner's sugar and continue beating on low for 2 more minutes until well blended.
6. Using a sandwich spreader or table knife, spread the strawberry cream cheese onto the rice cakes. Garnish each rice cake with a strawberry half.

Instead of cream cheese, you can use peanut butter.

CHAPTER 12

DISEASE FIGHTERS: FIVE A DAY FOR BETTER HEALTH

"Five a Day for Better Health" is a slogan being used all across the United States to encourage people to eat more fruits and vegetables. You may wonder why you need to eat more fruits and vegetables. It's simple: a diet high in fruits and vegetables helps reduce your risk of heart disease and cancer. In fact, your risk of cancer is cut in half when you eat five or more servings of fruits and vegetables daily. Fruits and vegetables are rich in vitamins, minerals, and fiber. They are almost all low in fat and calories.

A serving may be less than you think. One cup of leafy greens, as in a salad, or one-half cup of cooked vegetables makes one serving of vegetable. One medium piece of fresh fruit (such as an apple or banana), one-half cup of canned fruit, or three-quarters cup of juice count as one serving of fruit.

Want to take the Five-a-Day challenge? Try these 6 tips.

1. Add fruit to your cereal at breakfast.
2. Have lettuce and tomato, or any veggies you like, on your sandwich at lunch.
3. Drink juice instead of soda.
4. Eat fresh fruits as snacks.
5. Make a salad to go with your supper.
6. Pour canned fruit on frozen yogurt for dessert.

Now, let's make sure we all know how fruits and vegetables are different from each other. **Fruits** are the part of a flowering plant that contains the plant's seeds. Most fruits are juicy and sweet. Some fruits grow on trees, such as apples, pears, and cherries.

Vegetables are parts of plants that can be eaten, such as the plant's leaves, roots, or stems. For example, lettuce and cabbage are the leaves of plants, carrots are the roots, and celery is the stem. Most vegetables are not sweet.

Test your knowledge of fruits and vegetables in the following activity.

FRUIT OR VEGETABLE?

Purpose

To correctly identify fruits and vegetables.

Materials

notebook
red and green pencils

Steps

1. Write the following list of foods into your notebook:

broccoli
grapefruit
banana
corn
peas
apple
carrot
lettuce
potato
peach
tomato

2. Circle the fruits with the red pencil and the vegetables with the green pencil.
3. Check your answers below.

What Happened?

The following foods are fruits:

grapefruit

banana

apple

peach

tomato (surprise!)

The following foods are vegetables:

broccoli

corn

peas

carrot

lettuce

potato

See how easy eating Five a Day can be when you try out these delicious and nutritious recipes.

Quick and Easy Meat and Veggie Soup

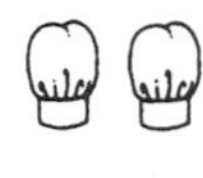

Time
25 minutes

Tools
large pot
fork
wooden spoon
colander
medium bowl
oven mitts

Makes
6 servings

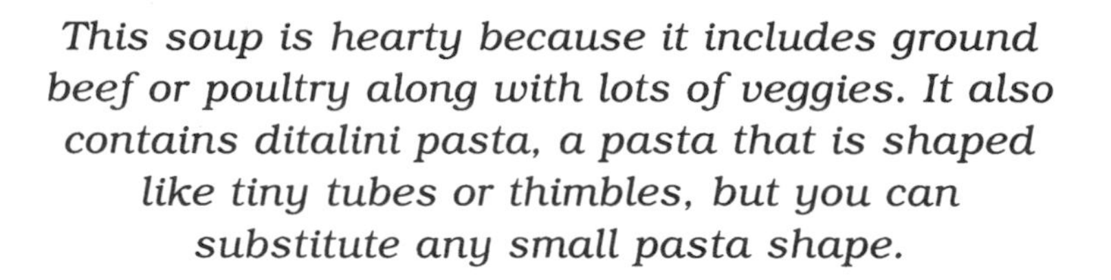

This soup is hearty because it includes ground beef or poultry along with lots of veggies. It also contains ditalini pasta, a pasta that is shaped like tiny tubes or thimbles, but you can substitute any small pasta shape.

Ingredients

- 1 tablespoon canola oil
- ½ pound lean ground chicken, turkey, or beef
- 3 cups canned beef broth
- 3 cups low-sodium tomato juice
- 1 cup water
- 1 teaspoon thyme
- ¼ teaspoon Worcestershire sauce
- 2 cups frozen mixed vegetables
- ¾ cup ditalini pasta
- 6 teaspoons grated Parmesan cheese

Steps

1. Put the oil in the pot over medium heat.
2. Add the ground meat and cook, breaking it up with a fork. Stir the meat with the wooden spoon until all of it is light brown and thoroughly cooked.
3. Place the colander over the bowl. Using oven mitts, drain the meat into the colander. Return the meat to the pot. Discard the fat.

4. Add the beef broth, tomato juice, water, thyme, and Worcestershire sauce to the pot. Bring the soup mixture to a boil.
5. Add the vegetables and pasta. Simmer the mixture for 8 to 10 minutes until the pasta is cooked.
6. Ladle the soup into bowls. Garnish each bowl with 1 teaspoon of grated Parmesan cheese.

Layered Vegetarian Bean Dip with Baked Tortilla Chips

Time
1 hour to warm cream cheese
plus
20 minutes

Tools
cutting board
paring knife
medium bowl
colander
wooden spoon
can opener
sandwich spreader
or
table knife
serving platter
or
large dinner plate

Makes
16 servings

This is a wonderfully spicy dip that is great as a snack.

Ingredients

- 2 8-ounce packages light or fat-free cream cheese
- ½ head lettuce
- 1 4½-ounce can chopped mild green chili peppers
- 1 31-ounce can refried beans
- 1½ cups reduced-fat shredded cheddar cheese
- ½ cup reduced-fat shredded Monterey Jack cheese
- 1 16-ounce jar mild salsa
- 1 16-ounce bag baked tortilla chips

Steps

1. Using the cutting board and paring knife, cut the cream cheese into 1-inch cubes. Put them in the bowl and set aside for 1 hour.
2. Place the lettuce in a colander and wash. Drain for 2 minutes.

Chili peppers range in flavor from mild to very, very hot. They are used in the cooking of Mexico and many Asian countries.

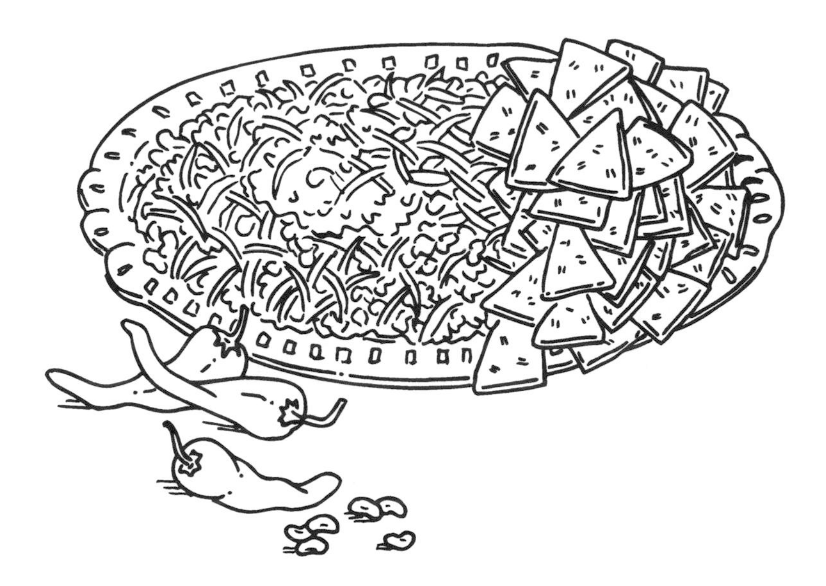

3. Lay the lettuce half flat side down on the cutting board. Cut the lettuce into ¼-inch strips. Set aside.
4. Mash the softened cream cheese by pressing it against the side of the bowl with the wooden spoon.
5. Open the can of chilies and drain. Add the chilies to the cream cheese and mix thoroughly for 5 minutes.
6. Using a sandwich spreader or table knife, spread the cream cheese mixture on the bottom of the large plate or serving platter.
7. Carefully spread the refried beans over the cream cheese.
8. Arrange a layer of lettuce over the beans.
9. Sprinkle both shredded cheeses over the lettuce.
10. Top with salsa.
11. Serve the dip with baked tortilla chips.

Pineapple-Raisin Sunflower Salad

Time
15 minutes

Tools
plate

cutting board

paring knife

ice cream scoop

Makes
1 serving

The ingredients in this recipe make the salad look like a sunflower in August! Make it as a side dish for lunch or dinner.

Ingredients

1 lettuce leaf

2 slices canned pineapple rings

1 scoop low-fat (2%) cottage cheese

½ cup raisins

1 teaspoon sunflower seeds

Edible sunflower seeds come from certain varieties of the sunflower plant.

Steps

1. Place the lettuce leaf on a plate.
2. Lay one pineapple ring in the center of the lettuce.
3. Using the cutting board and paring knife, cut the second pineapple ring into 8 equal pieces.
4. Lay pineapple pieces around the pineapple ring so that they look like flower petals.
5. Place a scoop of cottage cheese in the center of the pineapple ring.
6. Decorate the cottage cheese with the raisins to look like the center of a sunflower.
7. Sprinkle the salad with sunflower seeds.

Vitamin-Packed Wonton Cups with Roasted Vegetables and Cheese

***Wontons** are thin squares of dough usually filled with a small amount of meat, seafood, or vegetables. Wontons are popular in Oriental cooking. In this recipe, you will fill baked wonton wrappers with oven-roasted vegetables and cheese.*

Time
30 minutes to prepare
plus
1 hour to roast the vegetables

Tools
12-cup muffin pan
oven mitts
wire rack
cutting board
paring knife
large bowl
vegetable peeler
2 cookie sheets with sides
wooden spoon

Makes
12 wonton cups

Ingredients

- vegetable oil cooking spray
- 12 wonton wrappers or skins
- 2 carrots
- 2 red potatoes
- 1 red pepper
- 1 green pepper
- 1 small eggplant
- 1 onion
- ¼ cup olive oil
- 1 teaspoon dried basil
- 1 teaspoon dried oregano
- ¼ teaspoon salt
- ½ cup reduced-fat shredded mozzarella cheese
- 2 tablespoons dried parsley

Steps

1. Preheat the oven to 350°F.
2. Spray the muffin cups with vegetable oil cooking spray.
3. Carefully press a wonton skin to line the inside of each muffin cup.
4. Bake the wonton cups for 10 minutes or until light golden brown. Use oven mitts to remove the muffin pan from the oven. Allow to cool for 10 minutes. Carefully remove the wontons from the cups and place on a wire rack.
5. Wash and dry the carrots, potatoes, peppers, and eggplant. Remove the papery skin from the onion.
6. Using the cutting board and paring knife, cut the onion in half. Lay each onion half flat side down and cut into small pieces. Place in the large bowl.

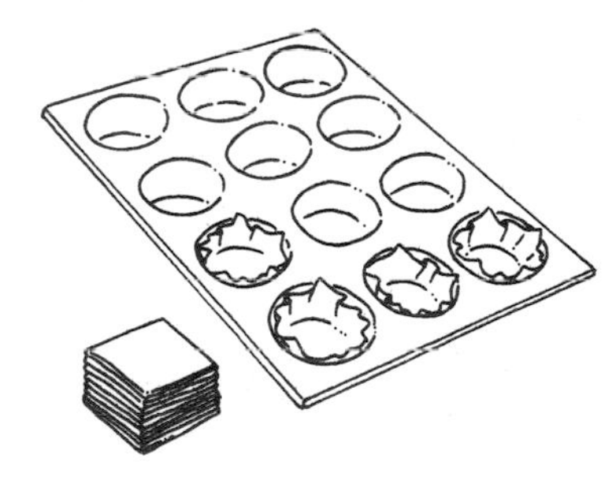

7. Peel the carrots with the vegetable peeler. Cut the carrots into ¼-inch slices and put them in the bowl.
8. Cut the potatoes into ½-inch slices. Cut each slice into ½-inch pieces. Put them in the bowl.
9. Cut the peppers in half and discard the seeds and white ribs. Cut each half into strips that are about ½-inch wide. Cut each strip into 1-inch long pieces, and put them in the bowl.
10. Wash and peel the eggplant, and cut it into 1-inch slices. Cut each slice into 1-inch cubes. Put them in the bowl.
11. Preheat the oven to 375°F.
12. Spray the cookie sheets with vegetable oil cooking spray.
13. Add the olive oil, basil, oregano, and salt to the vegetable bowl. Mix well with the wooden spoon. Turn the vegetable mixture onto one of the cookie sheets.
14. Roast the vegetables for 1 hour. Use oven mitts to remove the cookie sheet from the oven and allow it to cool on the top of the stove for 10 minutes.
15. Preheat the broiler. Fill the wonton cups with the vegetable mixture. Sprinkle lightly with cheese and parsley. Place 2 inches apart on the second cookie sheet.
16. Place the cookie sheet under the broiler until the cheese is melted and begins to bubble, about 1 minute. Keep your eye on the cups. Don't let the cheese brown.
17. Use oven mitts to take the cookie sheet out of the oven. Serve the vegetable cups as a lunch, hearty snack, or dinner side dish.

Oven-roasting vegetables brings out wonderful flavors

Tri-Berry Best Tartlets

Although this recipe calls for three types of berries, you can substitute any fresh fruit you like. Just cut it into bite-size pieces.

Time
15 minutes

Tools
colander
paper towels
cutting board
paring knife
medium bowl
wooden spoon

Makes
6 tartlets

Ingredients

- 1 cup raspberries
- 1 cup blueberries
- 1 cup strawberries
- 3 tablespoons sugar
- 6 individual graham-cracker tartlet shells
- 1 cup vanilla yogurt
- 6 mint leaves (optional)

Steps

1. Check the berries, and throw out the moldy ones. Then put all the good berries in the colander and wash them. Drain for 2 minutes. Pat dry with paper towels.
2. Using the cutting board and paring knife, cut the tops off the strawberries. Slice each strawberry lengthwise. Place in the bowl.

3. Add the raspberries and blueberries to the bowl.
4. Sprinkle the sugar on the berries. Mix gently with the wooden spoon.
5. Fill each tartlet shell with the berry mixture.
6. Top each tartlet with 1 heaping tablespoon of vanilla yogurt, and, with a mint leaf (optional).

NUTRIENT CONTENT OF RECIPES

This table shows the amount of calories, fat, cholesterol, fiber, and sodium contained in one serving of each recipe in this book. You can compare these numbers to how much you need daily as described in Appendix C.

Recipe	Serving Size	Calories	Fat (grams)	Cholesterol (milligrams)	Fiber (grams)	Sodium (milligrams)
Chapter 1 Have a Healthy Heart!						
Braided Breakfast Cinnamon Bread	1 slice (1/16th of loaf)	87	1	13	1	134
Tropical Chicken Kabobs	1 kabob	243	8	42	2	598
Honey-Raisin Pick-Me-Up Popcorn Snack	1/24 recipe	122	6	0	1	24
Meringue Shell Filled with Fresh Fruit and Frozen Yogurt	1/8 recipe	325	4	2	1	146
Cool-Down Watermelon Berry Drink	½ of recipe	259	4	11	1	69
Chapter 2 The Traveling Blood Show						
Individual Tex-Mex Meatloaves	1 each	350	24	120	0	376
One-Pot Creamy Navy Bean and Potato Soup	1½ cups	191	6	1	3	480

Recipe	Serving Size	Calories	Fat (grams)	Cholesterol (milligrams)	Fiber (grams)	Sodium (milligrams)
Dried Fruit and Nut Quick Energy Mix	¼ cup	144	8	0	2	6
Easy Cheese and Spinach Rice	¼ recipe	267	6	16	2	676
Chapter 3 Muscular Motions						
Hi-Pro Scrambled Eggs with Heart-Shaped Toast Cutouts	½ recipe	402	12	427	3	362
After-the-Workout Tuna Veggie Melt	1 muffin half	248	11	43	1	312
Crunchy Chicken Fingers	⅙ recipe	302	9	127	3	164
Tapioca Pudding and Tri-Berry Fruit Parfait	1 each	220	7	98	2	159
Pick-A-Flavor Power Boost Shake	½ recipe	242	7	6	0	95
Chapter 4 Long, Strong Bones!						
Wake-Me-Up Sunshine Salad	½ recipe	206	1	5	3	465
Garden Grilled Cheese Sandwich	1 sandwich	358	20	45	8	970
Bodacious Bok Choy and Beef	⅙ recipe	340	9	67	2	551
Creamy, Dreamy Yogurt Orange-Banana Frozen Pops	1 each	61	0	1	0	16
Chapter 5 "Look Mom, No Cavities!"						
Salsa Chicken	¼ recipe	242	11	88	0	407
Veggie Nibbles	½ cup	162	9	46	2	306
Swiss Cheese Salad	⅙ recipe	162	11	35	1	143

Recipe	Serving Size	Calories	Fat (grams)	Cholesterol (milligrams)	Fiber (grams)	Sodium (milligrams)
Apple Slices with Peanut Butter Dip	⅕ recipe	143	6	1	2	151
Chapter 6 Simply Radiant Skin, Hair, and Nails						
The Very Best Broccoli-Cheese Strata	⅙ recipe	352	14	169	4	701
Brown Sugar Sweet Potato Pie	⅛ recipe	331	14	81	2	318
Carrot Rounds with Orange Glaze	⅙ recipe	113	6	0	4	66
Awesome Cantaloupe Sorbet	¼ recipe	70	1	0	2	14
Strawberry-Kiwi Cooler	¼ recipe	118	2	5	1	33
Chapter 7 No-Stress Nerves						
Brunchtime Ham and Egg Croissant	¼ recipe	279	16	337	1	645
Fabulous Strawberry Crunch	⅙ recipe	281	9	0	6	108
Banana and Honey On-the-Go Bread	1 slice	191	9	27	2	240
Baked Buttermilk Spiced Donuts	1 each	89	1	1	1	49
Chapter 8 Moving Through the Digestive System						
Rise and Shine Raisin Bran Muffins	1 muffin	263	6	36	4	301
Mushroom Barley Soup	⅙ recipe	156	5	0	5	703
Hearty and Healthy Chicken Chili Stew	1 cup	262	11	55	4	579
Fiber-Rich Rice	¼ recipe	171	1	0	3	2

Recipe	Serving Size	Calories	Fat (grams)	Cholesterol (milligrams)	Fiber (grams)	Sodium (milligrams)
Autumn Apple Bread Pubbing	1/6 recipe	294	6	108	2	280
Peanut Butterscotch Popcorn Cutout Squares	1/30 recipe	159	10	2	1	33
Chapter 9 Enter the Food Guide Pyramid						
Breakfast No-Bake Granola Bars	1/18 recipe	153	4	0	1	90
Veggie Pockets	1 sandwich	142	1	0	3	616
Southwestern Macaroni and Cheese	1/8 recipe	333	10	50	6	460
Orange-Sauced Broccoli and Peppers	1/4 recipe	82	2	0	5	106
Gingersnappy Peach Crisp	1/6 recipe	163	4	0	0	59
Chapter 10 No More Couch Potato!						
Awesome Banana Berry Pancakes	1 pancake	176	7	36	2	106
Tricolor Spiral Pasta with Fresh Garden Veggies	1/6 recipe	489	16	0	1	185
Pick-Me-Up Power-Packed Lasagna	1/12 recipe	252	10	80	2	298
Energizing Apple-Oatmeal Squares with Raisins	1/12 recipe	343	13	54	6	206
Blueberry Power-Snack Turnovers	1 turnover	179	4	0	2	233

Recipe	Serving Size	Calories	Fat (grams)	Cholesterol (milligrams)	Fiber (grams)	Sodium (milligrams)
Chapter 11 Maintaining a Healthy Weight						
Trimline Blueberry and Nutmeg Muffins	1 muffin	148	5	18	2	144
Spicy Chicken and Cheese in Pita Pouch	1 sandwich	212	9	52	0	411
Fruit Combo Roll-Ups	1 roll	20	0	0	1	2
Rice-Cake Mini-Sandwich Snacks	1 sandwich	85	4	12	1	123
Chapter 12 Disease Fighters: Five a Day for Better Health						
Quick and Easy Hearty Veggie Soup	⅙ recipe	201	8	27	4	501
Layered Vegetarian Bean Dip with Baked Tortilla Chips	1/16 recipe	256	12	12	4	624
Pineapple-Raisin Sunflower Salad	1 serving	169	4	10	1	461
Vitamin-Packed Wonton Cups with Roasted Vegetables and Cheese	1 cup	140	6	3	2	91
Tri-Berry Best Tartlets	1 tartlet	204	9	2	2	162

HOW TO READ A FOOD LABEL

Ever notice that little section of the food label called Nutrition Facts on the foods you buy at the supermarket? Let's check it out—from top to bottom—on a frozen dinner.

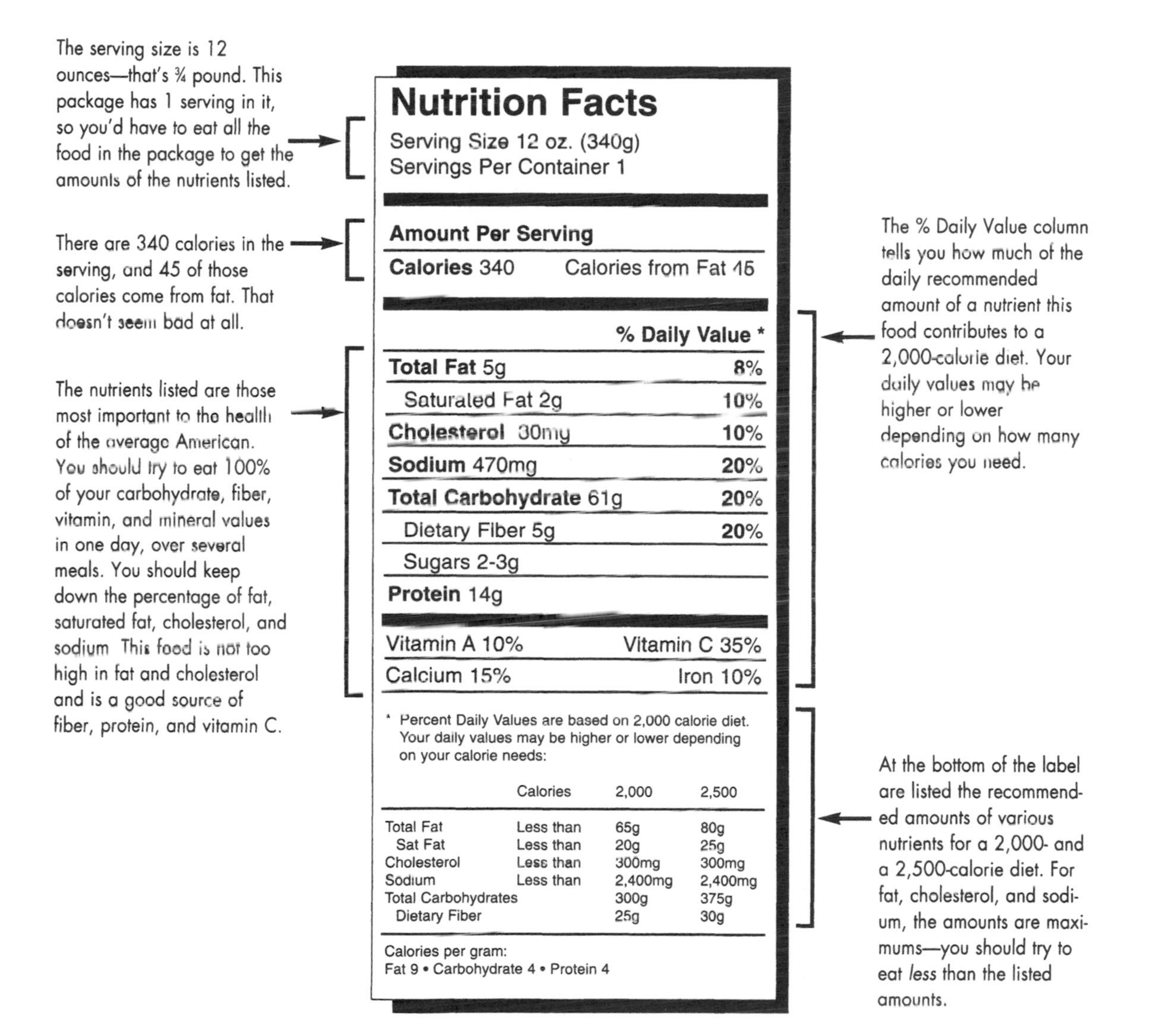

Nutrition Facts

Serving Size 12 oz. (340g)
Servings Per Container 1

Amount Per Serving

Calories 340 Calories from Fat 45

	% Daily Value *
Total Fat 5g	8%
Saturated Fat 2g	10%
Cholesterol 30mg	10%
Sodium 470mg	20%
Total Carbohydrate 61g	20%
Dietary Fiber 5g	20%
Sugars 2-3g	
Protein 14g	

Vitamin A 10% Vitamin C 35%
Calcium 15% Iron 10%

* Percent Daily Values are based on 2,000 calorie diet. Your daily values may be higher or lower depending on your calorie needs:

	Calories	2,000	2,500
Total Fat	Less than	65g	80g
Sat Fat	Less than	20g	25g
Cholesterol	Less than	300mg	300mg
Sodium	Less than	2,400mg	2,400mg
Total Carbohydrates		300g	375g
Dietary Fiber		25g	30g

Calories per gram:
Fat 9 • Carbohydrate 4 • Protein 4

WHAT'S SAFE TO EAT?

Even if you choose a very nutritious diet, there are still dangers lurking in your food. They seem to be reported on television and in the newspapers and magazines all the time. Are apples really sprayed with a dangerous chemical? Is eating an undercooked fast-food hamburger going to hospitalize you? Let's look at how to keep food safe.

FOOD POISONING

Foodborne illness, commonly called food poisoning, is caused by substances in food, such as bacteria and molds, which make you sick to your stomach but can be even more serious. Sometimes fever and infection occur. The symptoms may start within an hour of eating the suspected food or up to several days later.

Foodborne illness is most often caused by microorganisms. Microorganisms include bacteria and viruses. *Micro* means small, and both bacteria and viruses are so small that they cannot be seen by the naked eye. Bacteria are in the air, in the ground, and on you and me. Given the right temperature and enough time, bacteria will multiply in food (they double in number every 20 minutes). Bacteria cause foodborne illness when they multiply in food to the point that when the food is eaten, they make you very sick. Luckily, not all bacteria cause foodborne illness; only a small number do.

Bacteria grow readily under these three conditions.

1. **In a food that contains some protein,** such as meat, poultry, fish, eggs, dairy products, gravies and sauces, potatoes, beans, and rice.
2. **At a temperature between 40°F and 140°F.** Refrigeration is normally at or below 45°F, so bacteria grow slowly if at all. Bacterial growth slows down even more in the freezer, which is usually kept at or below 0°F. Room temperature is normally around 70°F—a great temperature for bacteria to grow.

3. **For at least 2 hours in the temperature zone given in # 2.**

In some, but not all, cases, adequate cooking of the contaminated food (to 165°F) will prevent problems. However, cooking does not kill all forms of bacteria, and in many cases the contaminated food may not even be cooked further, as in the case of tuna salad.

Here are some ways to prevent foodborne illness in your home.

1. Keep hot foods hot (above 160°F) and cold foods cold (below 45°F).
2. Wash your hands frequently, especially after handling raw meat, poultry, seafood, or eggs.
3. Don't touch yourself while handling food, because bacteria on your skin can then be introduced into the food. Don't use your fingers to taste food—use a spoon.
4. Cover all cuts, burns, and boils with a waterproof bandage. Cuts, burns, and boils are the home to many bacteria that you don't want in your food.
5. Keep all equipment sparkling clean and wash after every use. For instance, if you use your cutting board for cutting chicken, wash it thoroughly with *hot* water and soap before cutting lettuce on it (wash your knife, too)!
6. Use a different spoon for stirring raw foods, such as meat that is being browned, and cooked foods.
7. Cook and reheat foods until they are very hot and well done.
8. Don't eat raw meat, fish, or eggs. They may contain harmful bacteria, viruses, or parasites. If a dough or batter contains raw eggs, don't eat it before it is cooked!
9. Thaw meats, poultry, and seafood in the refrigerator overnight. Don't leave them out to thaw.

These are good rules to follow. A final rule of thumb is: "When in doubt, throw it out." It's probably not worth getting sick over.

MOLDS

Ever notice a little bluish green fuzz growing on your tomatoes? You probably knew it was just mold, but wondered if you could just cut out the moldy spot or if you should throw out the entire tomato. Molds cause spoilage (most often of fruits and bread), musty odors, and yucky flavors in foods. Molds also grow on vegetables, meats, and cheese that have been exposed to the air. Although molds will be killed by most cooking, the toxins (poisons) they produce will not, so you need to avoid eating moldy food. In foods with a firm texture, such as potatoes and hard cheeses, you can just cut out the moldy area. When dealing with a soft food, such as bread or tomatoes, it is best to throw the food out if you find any mold on it.

To avoid a dangerous mold that grows on peanuts (and corn), it is best to buy national brands. Also, throw out any moldy peanuts, peanut butter, cornmeal, or other corn products.

PESTICIDES

Pesticides are chemicals used to control insects, diseases, weeds, fungi, mold, and other pests on plants, vegetables, fruits, and animals. Pesticides are normally applied to crops as a spray, fog, or dust.

The government allows a small amount of pesticides to be left on the food you buy, but to be safe, you should avoid eating them. Here's how.

- Buy organically grown fruits and vegetables (these are grown without the use of pesticides) when possible.
- Throw away the outer leaves of leafy vegetables such as lettuce.
- Wash fruits and vegetables carefully, using a brush.
- Peel carrots, waxed cucumbers, peaches, and pears, because these foods are more likely to have hazardous pesticide residues.
- Buy local produce, as it is probably treated with less pesticide than produce that has to travel a long distance.
- Trim fat and skin from meat, poultry, and fish. Pesticides in animal feed can concentrate in animal fat. Skim fat from pan drippings, broths, sauces, and soups.
- Eat a varied diet so that no one food dominates.

GLOSSARY

absorption The process by which nutrients from food pass through the walls of the intestines into the blood.

arteries Large blood vessels that take blood containing oxygen away from the heart to the rest of the body.

B vitamins A group of vitamins that help keep the nervous system healthy.

backbone (or **spine)** The bones in the middle of your back that provide the central support for your body

bacteria Small microorganisms.

beat To move a utensil back and forth to blend ingredients together.

blend To mix two or more ingredients thoroughly until uniform.

blood A liquid that travels all around your body performing important jobs, such as carrying nutrients and body waste.

blood vessels Tubes that carry blood around the body.

boil To be at the boiling point—212°F or 100°C for water. When a liquid boils, that means it is turning into steam (the gaseous state of water).

bok choy A kind of Chinese cabbage with long, white stalks like celery and large, deep green leaves like spinach.

bone The dense, hard tissue that makes up your skeleton.

brain Part of your nervous system that is the control center for your body.

bran The outer layer of a grain, such as wheat. Bran is high in fiber.

calcium A nutrient that is needed for healthy bones.

calories A measure of the energy in food.

canines Teeth that are shaped like cones; they help spear and tear food.

capillary A very narrow blood vessel that connects arteries to veins.

carbohydrates A group of nutrients that includes sugars, starches, and fibers.

carbon dioxide A gas produced in the body that is pushed out when you exhale.

cardiac muscle A specialized type of muscle found in the heart. It contracts every second or so, yet never tires.

cavities (or **caries)** Holes that develop in teeth.

cells The building blocks of the body.

cholesterol A fatlike nutrient made in the body and found in every cell.

chop To cut into irregularly sized pieces.

circulatory system A system of the body that includes the heart, blood, and blood vessels.

coronary arteries Blood vessels that supply the heart with oxygen and nutrients.

cream To mix margarine or butter and sugar by pressing them against the bowl with the back of a spoon until they look creamy.

crisp A dessert made of fruit with a crumbly topping.

crown The part of the tooth that you can see.

deciduous (or **milk) teeth** Baby teeth.

dentin A substance like bone that is found in your teeth.

dermis The layer of skin found under the epidermis; it is packed with touch-detecting sensors.

dice To cut into cubes of the same size.

digestion The process during which food is broken down by the body into nutrients.

enamel The hard, protective surface that covers the crown of your teeth.

epidermis The protective outer layer of skin.

esophagus The tube that connects the mouth to the stomach.

fat A nutrient that supplies more energy than any other nutrient.

fiber A nutrient that makes you feel full. It is abundant in plant foods such as dried beans and peas, fruits, vegetables, whole grains, nuts, and seeds.

fibrin A substance found in the blood that helps blood clot.

fold To mix ingredients using a gentle over-and-under motion.

follicle A pit in the skin from which hair grows.

Food Guide Pyramid A guide to what you need to eat each day.

fruits The part of a flowering plant that contains the plant's seeds. Most fruits are juicy and sweet.

gastrointestinal tract The system of the body that digests food and absorbs nutrients.

grate To rub a food across a grater's tiny punched holes to produce small or fine pieces of food.

heart A muscle in the middle of your chest that pumps blood around your body.

incisors Teeth at the front of your mouth that are shaped like knives; they help cut and slice food.

integumentary system A system of the body that includes your skin, hair, and nails.

iron A nutrient that carries oxygen to the cells.

joints The places where bones meet, such as the knee joint.

kabobs Small pieces of meat, poultry, seafood, or vegetables placed onto a skewer, which looks like a stick.

keratin A tough material found in hair and nails.

knead To work dough into a smooth mass by pressing and folding with your hands.

large intestine Part of the digestive tract.

ligaments Strong structures that join bones together in joints and allow bones to move.

melanin A brown-black substance made by the skin that protects the skin from ultraviolet rays.

meringue A mixture of egg whites and sugar that is baked. It is a popular topping on pies, such as lemon meringue pie, but can also be baked as a pie shell.

mince To chop very fine.

minerals A group of nutrients that are needed for growth and good health.

mix To combine ingredients so that they are all evenly distributed.

molars Teeth in the back of the mouth that help crush and grind food.

muscle A tissue in the body that is responsible for moving parts of the body.

nerve cells Tissues in the body that are responsible for getting messages from the brain to the body and from the body to the brain.

nervous system A system of the body that includes the brain, spinal cord, and other nerve cells.

nutrient Substances in foods that are needed for you to grow, to repair your body, and to keep you healthy.

nutrition The science that explores the food you eat and how the body uses it.

oxygen A gas in the air that is necessary to support life.

pan-fry To cook in a pan over moderate heat in a small amount of fat.

pita bread A round, flat, Middle Eastern bread that forms a pocket when it is cut in half.

plasma A part of your blood that is mostly water, but also contains nutrients and other substances.

platelets A part of the blood that helps blood clot or stop bleeding.

potassium A mineral that is a nutrient.

premolars Teeth toward the back of your mouth that grind and crush food.

protein A nutrient that is needed for your body to grow and be healthy.

red blood cells A part of the blood that carries oxygen around the body.

reflex An automatic reaction such as moving your hand from a flame.

saliva A watery fluid released into the mouth when you put food in your mouth or even when you just smell food.

sauté To cook quickly in a pan over medium-high heat in a small amount of fat or liquid.

scab A blood clot that has dried and hardened on the skin.

shred To rub a food across a surface with medium to large holes or slits to produce small strips of food.

silken tofu A type of tofu. (See tofu.)

simmer To cook in a liquid that is just below boiling.

skeletal muscles Muscles that are usually attached to bones. They pull on your bones to make them move.

slice To cut into uniform slices.

small intestine Part of the digestive system.

smooth muscles Muscles found in the walls of blood vessels and in your stomach and other internal organs.

sorbet A frozen dessert similar to sherbet, except that sorbet is made with water, not milk.

spinal cord A thick bundle of nerves that goes from your brain down the middle of your back to a spot just below your waist.

spine (See backbone.)

steam To cook in steam.

stethoscope An instrument used to listen to sounds in the chest, such as heartbeat, and other parts of the body.

stomach A muscular sac that holds about 4 cups of food. Its job is to mix and mash up food.

strata A casserole usually made by layering bread, cheese, and other ingredients. An egg and milk mixture is then poured over the layers before the casserole is baked.

tofu A cheeselike food made from soybeans.

vegetables Parts of plants that can be eaten, such as the plant's leaves, roots, stem, or seeds.

vein Blood vessels that return blood to the heart.

vertebrae The bones that make up your backbone or spine.

vitamins A group of nutrients that are needed in small quantities for growth and good health.

whip To beat rapidly using a circular motion, usually with a wire whip, to incorporate air into the mixture (such as in making whipped cream).

whisk To beat ingredients together with a wire whip until they are well blended.

white blood cells A part of the blood that helps defend the body from intruders such as bacteria.

wonton A thin square of dough usually filled with a small amount of meat, seafood, or vegetables. Wontons are popular in Oriental cooking.

INDEX

C

D

E

F

G

H

I

M

N

O

U

V